T0196495

A CHILD
SPEAKS

A CHILD SPEAKS

A LONG JOURNEY HOME

DEE DEE BRUMM

iUniverse

A CHILD SPEAKS
A LONG JOURNEY HOME

iUniverse books may be ordered through booksellers or by contacting:

iUniverse
1663 Liberty Drive
Bloomington, IN 47403
www.iuniverse.com
1-800-Authors (1-800-288-4677)

ISBN: 978-1-5320-1741-4 (sc)
ISBN: 978-1-5320-1742-1 (e)

Library of Congress Control Number: 2017903118

Print information available on the last page.

iUniverse rev. date: 03/14/2017

Preface

This story reflects the many dilemmas that a child faces, among them
- dependency,
- desire for independence, and
- the frustrations brought on by adult views of the child.

A *Child Speaks* also examines the vulnerabilities of a child and makes clear that anger at a child only endangers the child's life.

Introduction

A Child Speaks is a true story told in the voice of the child involved. I've never been here before. My childhood came to an abrupt end. My life as it was came to an abrupt end.

Here is what happened.

- A visitor, saddened by war and his own mortality, needed cheering. I missed my dad, who was away at war. I wanted to cheer the visitor the way my dad cheered me.
- I told the visitor a funny story, one dad had often told. I almost never tell jokes because I can't make them seem funny. I did then tell my father's story, though.

  It was a story about a dog looking for a fireplug and not quite making it. I then squirted a little liquid I held in my hand on the visitor's hand.
- After telling the story, the visitor showed me a story with his private part, and my world was never the same.

  I left my mind that day, and nothing afterward was quite the same.
- Later, the visitor played versions of his story on me whenever he could and wherever on my body he could. Each time it happened, I would leave my mind. It seemed that less of me came back each time.
- Then, if that were not enough, our family went to visit the man when my dad came back from the war. And I met others on that mind path away also.

- And later the visitor came to visit us with his new wife and to meet my new brother. The visitor visited upon my new brother too, and there was nothing I could do.
- A little time passed, and again we went to visit the visitor. But now I was angry at the experiences and beat upon him as he visited upon my brother.
- The visitor unleashed further attacks, and I slipped into deeper mental realms. I went far away and returned with even less of me.
- The visitor raged at me and threw words about to destroy me, and when that was not enough, the visitor tried to totally destroy me. By the grace of an angel, the visitor only left my brain in unmatchable pieces. And so I was left with what seemed like pieces of my mind that could never be put back together and the traces of images left behind after the loss of a mind.

Chapter 1

I didn't know I was an adult survivor. I didn't know what an adult survivor was. "What does that mean?" I asked.

Yes, I am over twenty-one years old. Yes, I am alive and able to write this account. Does that make me an adult survivor?

It was late one night. I remember going into my mother's bedroom, and there she was, lying on the bed crying. She just lay there, stretched out like Wendy in *Peter Pan*. Her satin gown lay smoothly around her and on the bed, as if placed there perfectly. Her bare feet were just lying there. I could hear the sound of crying, crying in the stillness.

Where was she? I know—she was lying on the bed. But where was she? She certainly didn't seem like she was in the present. It looked like her mother was dreaming except that she was crying.

My own dilemma was just as strong.

I knew something was wrong. The visitor had done something to me. He had touched me. He had something attached to him that he touched me with.

I was sore now. I had felt tingly then. I didn't know what to do. It frightened me. I had fled, or so it had seemed. I wasn't there mentally after a while. I played as if it weren't happening. It. It. What he touched me with was big—it was huge and strong, and it had hurt.

I hadn't been aware before that there was a hole there in the bottom of my body. It was a hole like the one Alice in Wonderland fell down.

I had tried to escape but was somehow tied down and could not escape. It was so quiet and lonely. I was lost. Where was I? Oh, now it came—the pain. Why? Why was this sad man hurting me? Where could I go?

He picked me up and seemingly brushed me off.

He spoke to me. "Now, now, you're all okay, just like your pretty little dolly here. See, she's smiling at you. See, she says, "Hi, Maria.

"Come play with me.

"Come play."

He hands me the doll, putting her in my arms and placing my arms around her. He strokes my hair and forehead while humming a little sweet melody.

*****I try to escape but find I am somehow tied down and cannot escape. It is so quiet and lonely.

I am lost. Where am I?

Oh, now it comes - the pain. Why? Why is this sad man hurting me? Where can I go?

"There, there. The doctor makes you all better now," he seemed to be saying to the doll.

I wake up. The room is dark. My lower area hurts. Why does it hurt? It's sore and seems to thump—no, throb.

She wakes now, alone and in the dark – a new scene.

I am afraid. I'm sure there is something hiding in the dark there by the floor where my toys are. I must not go down there. How will I step by them? Mother will be mad that the toys are on the floor. But I'm afraid there's something on the floor. Somehow I slide off the bed and inch by the toys and run out of the room in search of mother, screaming.

She's in the living room mending something and talking to the soldier man. She's very pretty in the soft light. He is quietly looking at her. I burst into the scene, screaming. She seems distracted and looks at him first before looking at me.

She seems to be wondering what has prompted this outburst. She slowly puts her mending on the table beside her and beckons me to get on her lap. She calmly asks me what is wrong, but I am now self-conscious and aware of his eyes on me in the room.

He does not seem so sad and quiet and unhappy as he did in the afternoon before what he called "the games." I feel his eyes going to me, and there is some strange power or force that I fear. I don't know this feeling. I don't recognize it, but I feel it as if it was a grip, a strong and powerful grip almost immobilizing me.

He is across the room sitting quietly, not making a motion or a move or a sound. I can sense his breathing, and I am scared.

Mother is trying to talk to me. At first, I do not hear her. She seems to be getting annoyed, impatient. The room is only semilit; dark shadows are cast about on the walls from the light of the big fire ablaze in the fireplace. Strange. Daddy doesn't allow fires in the fireplace very often. Why does she have one now?

"Maria, you're not answering me! What's wrong? Why aren't you in your bed and asleep?" Her voice is getting sharp and strained. I can feel her impatience with me.

She puts me down and moves slowly out of the big old armchair with wings. She moves the hair out of my face with her hand and then takes my chin and grips it and tilts my head so she can look straight at me. "Maria, it's back to bed. I won't have any nonsense."

It is just as we reach the hallway to the bedroom that I remember why I came screaming into the living room and why I don't want to go back into the bedroom and to the monsters lurking there.

Mother is smiling now. Relieved. *It was only a child's nightmare. She's probably just missing her daddy. He spoiled her so.*

It is morning now. The sun streams into the kitchen window. The visitor, Ray, is taking us on a drive to the lake.

Mother is quietly thinking, *"I'll have to get Maria dressed. She's so agitated. Last night, she was impossible, bursting in on a lovely evening of music and dreaming.* Ray had built a big fire in the fireplace. *He is a silly, sentimental man.* It was really too early for a fire. The days were still quite warm, but it made him happy, and he seemed quite determined. *It is so nice to have an attentive handsome man around again.*

What again? I feel so special with him. Silly me."

But Ray was such a hero, and her letters meant a lot to him, especially in the hospital after the rescue in Egypt. His presence was so strong. She could sense his approach, his hand on her shoulder.

She heard him saying, "I'll take care of Maria. She's daydreaming. I love helping little girls get dressed."

She smiled. It was a relief to just sit here and enjoy the pampering. He was such a natural with children.

*****

I'm sitting amid my dolls arranging a tea party when he enters the room. Mother's mood seems to have carried over to me, and I am humming a tune. The room is filled with light.

Then he comes and stands over me, and I sense a dark shadow.

Chapter 2

Hello, Hello. Where am I? I don't know. I'm just a child. Who knows?

"I don't know," said the rabbit to the hare.

"Funny, bunny."

"What's so funny?" said the rabbit to the hare.

"Everyone knows the rabbit is a hare. Silly."

I curl up in the chair beside him while he reads.

Mother is smiling again. I smile too. He is a silly man. Yet in the room, it is different, so different. I like him out here, and he makes me laugh. Strange that he is not so sad now. Was I wrong to tell him the story to make him not sad?

My mind wanders. He is reading again:

"The Brook and the Fox."

What did he say? The Brook and the Fox?

No. The Box and the Fox.

"Look, the fox is in the box."

Stupid. Silly. Giggle, giggle.

He tickles me. My skin tingles. I am mixed all over. It sends a smile to my face. Mother is in her chair sewing. She is absorbed somehow yet still humming. Strange. Here we are with this man. Strange.

Where are we? Hello, hello.

"Can you write?"

"Yes. See, I can do the alphabet."

"Bright girl. You'll go far."

"Where?"

"Where do you want to go?"

"Home."

"You are at home, young lady," mother responds.

"No, I'm not. I'm not home."

"What are you talking about?"

"I'm not home."

"Yes, you are.

"Now stop that right this minute! Go on now and wash your hands. It is time for supper."

"Can I sing for my supper?"

"No, I've had enough of your nonsense for one day. If you are not careful, I'll put you to bed now, and you won't get to eat with uncle Ray."

He's uncle now. I bet she'd like for me to act up and go to bed now. Should I? Shouldn't I? Oh, well, washing hands.

Ray enters the bathroom behind me.

"Hello, young lady. You're quite a young lady, you know. Here let me dry your hands."

He closes the door. I feel him take my pants down. He kisses me there. I'm all tingly. I wiggle to get away. He grabs me and pulls me back. One hand pushing deep into my arm, with the other hand, he pulls up my pants and swats my behind.

"Now, don't you tell. Your mother will give you what for."

It seems like a game, yet … I kick at him under the table, swinging defiantly, but mother sees me swinging my feet, and explodes. "No supper."

*****

6

The room is dark. The scary things are out. I listen, but I cannot hear. I feel like a Raggedy Ann doll. Not a real person but a Raggedy Ann doll – something to be played with and manipulated. Tears. Bad heart. I don't know. I don't know.

I play pretend under the covers. I don't like the feelings in the dark. I want it all to stop.

I yell, "Stop. Stop. Stop."

Mother hears me and yells into the room, "Quiet, Maria. Shush, now. Go to sleep."

Ray offers to just peek in on her.

He enters the dark room, switches on the light and switches it off again.

He lets mother know she's okay.

"Thanks, Ray."

He speaks to mother. "I'll just be a few moments. I'm going to sit by her for a few minutes. You just relax."

"Thanks."

He closes the door gently and walks over to the bed where I am sitting up.

He puts his hand up to indicate I should shush and lays me back down. He puts his lips on mine. I turn and twist. He takes his hand and puts it below. My body tingles, again and again, while he is saying, "That's not so bad."

I'm choking and try to bite his hand. I try to wiggle, but I can't. Then I leave. He is pushing on me, again. I feel strange and sick at the same time. He puts his hand back over my mouth.

"Now, now. Don't cry. You'll be all right. You know you wanted me to do that, right? Right. Oh, my dear little girl. We'll play our game, won't we! We'll play a game of seek but do not tell. See I seek …"

He runs his fingers all over me, almost tickling me.

"You won't tell."

He presses his hand on my arm and again does it to me. I am in pain. The tears stream. I bite my lip. I feel shame. That's the name of his game—shame, shame, shame, shame on you ... Button my shoe. Cows in the meadow. Won't get you.

I imagine a jump rope goes over and over me. I trip. I'm out. What? Where am I?

"Hello, hello?" I feel sick. "Hello?"

It's dark and quiet now. I listen. I slowly slide out of bed. I sit on the floor, too sore to move. My legs feel weak. There is something wet on me, from my legs, running down. I touch it. It is cold and sticky. I roll around on the rug to wipe it off. Ugh. I roll and roll and fall asleep.

*****

There is no tomorrow, no today. In my dreams, I imagine I am picked up by my daddy, put back to bed, covered, tucked in, and touched on the forehead. But no, it was not daddy. It was the man with no feeling for me.

I feel like a heavy bag he puts to bed. I hit my head. He moves it about like rubber. He looks over me. I freeze. I am frightened. I don't know. What? What? I feel empty and sick. I don't know this feeling. I'm sick. He's upset. I throw up. Where's mother? It's so quiet out there. I'm sick. Does she know? Does she know I'm sick?

"Mommy. Mommy."

"Quiet, Maria. You'll be all right. You have a doctor to take care of you. You'll be all right.

"She will be all right, won't she?"

"Not to worry. Just a toy she was chewing on."

"Oh, dear. What am I to do?"

I'm only somewhat here, hearing, yet wanting mother, not Ray. Why doesn't she come?

"You'll get well. Shush, shush. Just don't tell."

The night is dark. The door is closed.

I want to cry out that I won't get well.

I will go to hell. Down, this is a very bad down.

The next morning, Ray and mother can be heard talking.

"Where is Maria?"

"She's asleep."

Mother enters the bedroom, still talking to Ray. "Maria has to get up. She's probably just moping around."

"Come on, Maria, put your feet on the ground. Get up. Let's put this dress on. Easy does it. Over your head. Maria, stop wiggling around. Take your hands out of your undies. There, don't do that. Come on. I'll brush your hair. You have pretty, silky hair."

"I don't."

"Do not. Yes, you do."

"Don't."

"Do not. Maria, really, you're quite impossible, you know."

"Ouch, that hurts."

"That's not all that will hurt if you don't sit still while I tie your hair. Now, hold still."

"Yes, ma'am."

"Don't you 'yes, ma'am' me. It's, 'Yes, mother, I will obey. Yes, mother, I will be good today.'

"Now, young lady, I don't want any of your shenanigans today. Your misconduct is unfitting for a young lady, and I will not have it, you hear?"

"Yes, ma'am."

"What?"

"Yes, mother. I'll be good."

"That's right. That's more like it. Now, go give uncle Ray a big hug and kiss."

"Do I have to?"

"Why, yes, of course, silly girl. He's taken very good care of you."

"Oh. All right.

"Good Morning, Ray," I say, with eyes averted.

He takes me by the chin, and sees that there are tears.

He averts his eyes and goes on with his reading, turning away from me.

Devastation. Mother senses I have offended him, somehow. This is bad.

Mother speaks up. "I won't have it. Young lady, you march up to Ray right this minute and apologize. Tell him you are sorry and give him a kiss."

I am feeling all aflutter and confused. Yet as I near him, I feel tingly again by my legs and wet my pants.

I am so unhappy. I cry. I wee. I feel lost. Why? Why? It runs down my legs and into my socks and shoes.

Mother grabs me and rushes me to the bathroom. She is bewildered. "What can I do, Maria? What is going on? I am so sick and tired of all this. Hold still. Behave. Be quiet."

Mother speaks out. "Why me, Lord? Why this thankless, ugly child? She's her father's child, not mine. Oh, dear."

She cleans me up, talking all the while. I'm exhausted, and it's only morning. I want to lie down. I break loose from her and run to my room and lay across the bed, sobbing.

Ray intercepts mother as she starts toward Maria. "Just let her be. She'll be all right. Come, let's go outside and enjoy the day. I have something to say. He draws her near. She starts but does not pull away. He takes her hand and pats it gently. She almost lays her head against him. Her body relaxes. They are sitting on the daybed on the screened porch. He fiddles with her hair. He looks at her.

"Frances, you know I care deeply for you."

Mother seems to sense it. She sighs and smiles and thinks of the evening by the fire before Maria interrupted it.

I wish that child would go away.

Ray is fiddling with her tie at the neck of her blouse.

The dark green shade is partially down on the front of the screen porch, shielding the windows from the bright morning sun.

She runs her hand back and forth along the cord of the daybed cover, sort of caught in limbo, wondering, yet not thinking what to do. She senses his presence, his move. She is overwhelmed by a sense of emotion, of longing that swells in her throat. She starts to speak, but no sound comes out.

He is watching, silently, the whole time. His heart is pounding. He draws her near. He takes her head in his hand and presses her lips to his, in a strong, sustained kiss.

Maria is standing, watching through the blinds of the long, low window, which looks out onto the screened porch, beside where the daybed is placed. She feels some strange jolt, as if the wind has been knocked out of her. She does not speak. An anger and rage wells up. She does not want what Ray does, but senses mother is taking him away. She stares at the scene, yet tries not to see.

Mother speaks to Ray. "What do you want?"

"See what you have done to me."

He puts her hand on him. She pulls back. She is hesitant.

"I can't help it. You are so much to me. Help me."

"Help you?"

"Yes, touch me."

She shakes, her body pulsing. They kiss. He moves toward her legs. She starts to pull back.

He pushes her to her knees. "Help, help me," he pleads.

Mother is distracted. I pull away but remain watching from the window. They kiss again. She puts her hands on his chest. His body shivers. She is most tenuous in her touch and reticent about the emotions within. They are entwined. They are kissing. At the same time, she is fighting back tears. He bites her lips. He maneuvers her onto the bed, lowers the side shades to the neighbors, lifts her skirt, and kisses her tummy, her breasts. He, ever in control, pushes her loose-legged pants aside. She starts to scream. He kisses her. She is responsive. He rubs his part, now out of his slacks, against her. He rubs again and again as she touches his tight, muscular body, as they are made one.

Maria watches from the vantage point, on a chair, where she can see, through the drawn blinds. She has seen this with daddy, but it wasn't the same. And she knows, somehow, this is what Ray is doing to her. Her mouth feels strange. She steps down from the chair, moves it back in place. She tiptoes out of the room and back to her own bed, where she lies down, her hand between her legs and rocks to sleep.

Chapter 3

It was the next day. Mother was up late. She was singing. She was happy. She was joyful. She was in a good mood. I ventured into the kitchen. I smiled, hopeful of a loving, friendly response.

"Gotcha," came the response, but not from mother. It was Ray, from the corner of the kitchen, grabbing me and swinging me up and sitting me down in my chair. He smiled at her, and she smiled back.

"Maria, pull your hair back. It'll get in your food."

Ray continued to be all energy, keeping up the energy for me and for mother, who still hummed to herself while stirring the oatmeal. Toast popped up. The sun filtered in through the kitchen window, hitting the blue glass bottle with the round base and the skinny, long neck. It cast a pattern of blue light in a small path along the floor. I watched it for a while.

"Maria, stop daydreaming and eat your toast."

"I'm not hungry," I replied, upset to be disturbed in my watching of the blue light pattern.

Ray recognized my gaze and moved the vase just slightly so that the blue hit the table. He then moved the plate of toast so that it sat where the blue light fell, except the blue light couldn't really be seen on the toast, as if absorbed by it. I picked up the toast and began eating.

"Don't play with your food, young lady."

Mother was definitely from a different planet. Ray got up and whispered something in mother's ear while she stood by the stove. She smiled slightly but turned to give me a hard stare as I watched from the table.

"Well, young lady, are you ready for an excursion today? Uncle Ray has gotten us a car, and we're off to see what we can see. And there are further treats; you'll see.

"Maybe we can leave her home. Perhaps we can. I'll check with Mary. You like Mary and Jack, don't you, Maria?"

Ray was quiet, too quiet.

"I'll go and see if Mary can help."

Mother put down her apron and went out through the dining room to the living room, opening the front door.

"I'll be right back. If the water starts to boil over, just turn it off."

The quiet was deafening. Ray reached over the table, and touched my hand. He turned it over and traced the story I had told him, casually, around my palm.

First the tree and then the telephone pole and then the fire hydrant. He then pressed his thumb into the center of my palm and closed my hand around it. I was devastated. I could not think. I wet my panties. I ran to the bathroom, afraid I might be punished. Ray was wiping off the plastic on the seat as mother came back in.

"Just a little accident. She'll need clean undies, I suspect."

"That does it. I'm not taking any child of mine who wets her pants into someone else's car, where she might wet again. I just won't have it."

She turns to see me at the corner of the room.

"Mary said you could come, Maria, and keep her company while she bakes for John. You'll enjoy that. You always do.

"Now, no more whimpering. Let's put on that new dress and a diaper so that Mary doesn't have to worry."

"I won't wet."

14

"How do you know that? You can't promise that."

"Yes, I can. Please, mommy."

"Don't 'Mommy' me! We'll see, when we're ready to go."

Ray was very quiet, not looking anywhere. He got busy with the newspaper, folding it up. He cleared the table and moved on out of the room to fold up his clothes and blankets and move them off the couch in the living room. There were remains of ashes, from the night before, in the fireplace.

*****

I thought of all the leaves out at the park that I had kicked, while walking through them, with daddy, the autumn before. It made me think of daddy and feel sad that he was not there. He would take me along. Daddy had been sad that day in the park. He'd let me kick the leaves.

After a while, I took his hand, while kicking the leaves.

"Daddy?"

"Yes, sweetheart?"

"Why are you so sad?"

"Your daddy's worried; that's all. He has a lot on his mind."

"I'll take care of you, daddy."

"I know you will, sweetheart. Here, let me pick you up. Maybe, you can reach that pretty leaf up there, to take home to your mother."

"I don't want to."

"Why not?"

"Mommy made you sad, didn't she?"

"Well, your mother and I don't see eye to eye on something."

"What do you mean, daddy?"

"Well, your mother wants to go back home to her family."

"But we're her family, aren't we, daddy?"

"Yes, sweetheart."

His attention seemed to drift off again, and I returned to kicking leaves. He stopped suddenly, knelt down, and pulled me around, almost setting me on his bent knee. "You know, I love you, very, very much, my precious, little Maria Dee."

He smiled at hearing his words and then looked seriously at me for my response.

"Oh, yes, daddy," I said, giving him a big hug.

With that, he picked me up and put me on his shoulder, running around and about.

"Good," he said. Then he stopped, a bit short of breath, putting me down and taking my hand.

"We must get back to mother and see what she has for us to eat."

I remembered the night before, hearing her crying. "I want to go home. I'm no good at this. I just can't do it. I want to go home."

"But I can't leave Texas. It's my job."

"I know."

Daddy had taken a job and been transferred to Texas. Now, however, in the war, he had to also serve in the army.

"Please stay here. Take care of the house. Take in boarders, if you like, but, please, don't leave."

"That's not the point."

"I know, but now is not the time, with the war and all."

"It's precisely the time. I want to go home."

"What about Maria Dee?"

"I'll take her with me, of course."

"But—"

"Chris, I'm serious about this."

"I know."

Later that night, I awoke, and climbed down from my bed, holding on to the railing, and tiptoed over to their big bed. I climbed up the chest and into the bed and the space between them, as I was want to do when something awoke me in the night. They were turned away from each other. There was a sad, sad feeling here. Before, when here, I felt warm and secure. This feeling now was frightening. I fell asleep, crying, overwhelmed by the feeling of emptiness between them.

*****

Mother was waiting, impatiently, for me to put my shoes on to go to Mary's house. I had chosen the buckle ones, so that I could show Mary. Mother wasn't happy about this, but she looked at me and bent over to help. She was not so happy at the moment, as she had been in the kitchen. The conversation with Mary had upset her.

"I told your mother to be careful. What would people say if they saw her out with some strange man?"

"He's not some strange man. He's daddy's best man's brother and a war hero."

"Yes. Yes. But all the same, it's best to be careful. You have to live around here, and people will talk.

Well, young lady, what are we going to bake for John today?"

"A peach pie?"

"Well," she said, smiling, "I know what your favorite is, but it's too late for peach pie."

"How about apricot?"

"I'm afraid it's too late for that too."

I was beginning to be upset. Why had she asked me, anyway? I started looking around the kitchen, opening cupboards. She had rows and rows of metal-looking pans, and all were arranged in some sort of order.

She asked, if I wanted to take the pans out and put them on the floor and then, play with them.

I didn't respond, so she got papers out, laying them on the floor and indicated which cupboards I could explore by opening the doors.

"Now, leave these others shut, while I work on supper."

I noticed she was snapping beans.

"I can do that." I left the pans on the floor.

"Okay. But first, pick up the pans."

That was more of a challenge than I'd first expected. But with only one correction, I managed to get them back in order. I was most pleased. She put an apron around me, which came almost to my ankles and tied it up under my arms. I was allowed to stand on a chair, to lean over to reach the beans, and to help break them into a heavy, beige bowl with a red band around it. I watched ever so carefully not to put stems in the bowl, but in the throw away pile, with the strings, which occasionally surfaced when I broke the beans. I was happy and singing, while Mary chatted away about what people say.

Chapter 4

It was nighttime, and Ray was reading a story to Maria. She'd wiggled uncomfortably when being placed in his lap, embarrassing Frances, who is now doing mending. It would seem a domestic scene, only she was crying. Chris had called.

Chris had said "I love you, dear, dearest Frances. I love you. Please, dear, dearest Frances, please be faithful. I love you. I love you. Please, be true. I love you. I will make it up to you. You will see. We'll have a son of our own, one of your own choosing.

"I love you. I miss you. I hope all is well.

"Give Maria Dee a big hug for me. Oh, that she could climb up on my knees and sit in my lap. Oh, oh, I do miss my girls so very much.

"Dear, dearest Frances, please be true. I do love you."

After his call and letter, the tears continued to well up inside Frances's delicate frame. It shook her suddenly, like a cold wind—a draft of things to come, foreseen. Had she been hasty? Had she been mean? No. He had taken her away from all she knew. What was she to do? Encourage him? No. It wouldn't do. Would he take her back with him? *I don't know.*

She suddenly realized she was not thinking of Chris, whose letter and call had brought her to tears. She was thinking of Ray, so near to her.

He was reading to Maria, yet giving her his prioritized attention. She liked that about him. He was most attentive to Maria Dee, although there seemed to be some friction there. Even with his attention there, he remained aware of her, of her needs. It was so, so hard to admit, to compare. It was so welcomed to not allow other thoughts to take rein.

"And then, the big, bad wolf said, 'What fine teeth you have, Granny.'"

"No. No. No. He didn't say that. Granny said that, not the wolf. You made that up."

Ray smiled at his little Maria. *Nice scene*, he thought. *That Frances is a complex one.* She was certainly supportive. Frances had been most attentive today along the drive and in the park. He thought of the kisses, freely given and with great hunger.

Easy boy. You'll get your own. Easy. Soon, soon, soon. I promise. Great pleasure.

And a jewel, sits upon my lap. Heaven. Let's see. Perhaps it was time for a nap or a story in bed.

Hmm.

It was later in the evening, and he and Frances were sitting on the couch together looking at a scrapbook of pictures of her family, her wedding, and her move to Texas. He reached over, puts his hand across the page, and then turned her face toward him.

"I am jealous of every moment not shared with you, Frances." Looking into her face and dark, brown eyes, he saw she was trembling.

"Ray, do you care the least for me?"

"Oh, yes, yes. You know, I do."

His head moved closer to hers, their lips almost touching. He inserted his tongue into her mouth, touching her tongue. At the same moment, their lips moistly, gently touched, sending spasms of desire through their bodies. They were entwined with passion. Ray quickly moved the dress shoulder down her arm and reached quickly to her left breast, kissing it passionately, while moving her dress further down. She was engulfed in passion and desire, the fire's glow warming the scene.

Maria was watching, at a diagonal from the door of the kitchen, which led to the dining room and then, through an archway to the living room and the couch, shaped like a sleigh bed.

*****

Maria Dee was standing, barefoot, on the cold kitchen floor, beside the stove. She had wanted a drink of water and had intended to push a chair up to the sink to get a glass and water. However, as she tiptoed into the kitchen, to see if the coast was clear, she could see her mother and Ray on the couch, his hand on her thigh and her mother struggling to break free. She accidently hit his cheek and pulled back in horror.

That's what Maria Dee wanted to see. She felt very, very sick in the stomach as she watched her mother and Ray, in an activity she had seen mother and daddy in once, and recognized that it was somewhat like what Ray was doing when he played his game with her, only it was different. Mother was different with Ray. She was doing it with him.

She, Maria, felt sick in the stomach. She didn't know why. She sat down on the kitchen floor. She turned around and crawled farther back into the kitchen. She bit her lip until it bled. Her nose began to run. She tried to keep quiet, fighting the tears. She didn't understand. Why was he hurting her? And, also, why was he hurting her mother?

She wiped her nose on her sleeve and crawled back, to the doorway to look again. Mother's back was arched as she lay on the couch, pulling Ray to her. He was kissing her, kissing her neck and cheeks and her mouth as he moved back and forth on her. She was all involved, and her skin glistened with the reflection of the fire.

They lay side by side on the couch, stroking each other and talking softly.

Ray had, earlier, stepped beside the couch to open the lid of the large music box and, with her instructions, had wound the box to play music. Now they lay there, side by side, listening and drifting away.

Maria too was getting very sleepy and moved quickly to the bathroom and back to bed, leaving the door slightly ajar so as not to make any sound.

Ray was awakened from his revere by the sound of Maria getting into bed. He quickly arose from the couch, covering himself with his robe and gently kissing Frances awake.

"Frances, I hear the sound of little feet. Better interrupt this dream and move to bed. Do you want me to help you," he said with a smile.

"No." She smiled back. "I don't think so." She was in a state of great content as she made her way to the front bedroom. Frances is hoping Chris will come to take Maria.

Ray looked in on her, turned off the light, and closed the door. After going to the bathroom, he walked quietly into the back bedroom, looking behind to make sure the door to the front bedroom was really closed. He then tiptoed over to Maria's bed, where she lay, playing like she was asleep. He pulled the cover down and moved in beside her for a moment.

She held herself tight. He put his hand between her legs, and they were wet. He pulled the cover back. Tears ran down her cheeks. Her stomach was a mess. She was frightened and confused.

He spoke. "My dear, little Maria, did you see your mother and me?"

She tensed up, fearful.

"Ah, you did. But you know I love you, don't you? Haven't I told you? Haven't I played with you?"

Passion raged through her little body. She was confused by the feelings she felt and the feelings she had seen. She only knew her feelings and the confusion.

"Don't you worry," he said, rubbing the skin between her legs with his part. "I'll play with you again. And I'll— Hmmm, what's this? Big bear is getting bigger and going to get you."

He entered her, pushing again and again. She felt lost, losing herself, with only her body feelings there. Where was she? Where did she go? She felt sick in the stomach. She didn't understand. She lay there with him beside her, wondering what this was all about, yet feeling very, very sick in the stomach.

Sometime in the night, he tiptoed out of the room and down the hall, gently opening the door ajar to the front bedroom, where Frances lay asleep in much the same position as before. He returned to the bathroom, washed up, turned out the light, and returned to the couch. The embers of the fire were still burning.

He lit a cigarette—knowing it was against house rules. He chuckled to himself about the house rules, knowing they were meant to be broken. All in all, a fine day for himself had been had. Perhaps his return to life was more promising than he had previously thought.

He put out the cigarette, threw the ashes into the fireplace, and returned to the couch and to sleep, to awaken to the smell of pancakes, in the kitchen, and the sight of Maria and Frances working together in the kitchen.

"Will Ray stay?" Maria asked.

Mother responded, "I don't know, sweetheart. Maybe soon."

Chapter 5

Daddy came home from the war the next spring. I could hardly wait. I was so excited. I loved talking with him. I loved sharing with him. It had always been that way. But it was not as before. He was more silent, less sharing.

His heart was not there, and yet he was there. He was home. I was most excited. I loved my daddy very, very much, and, until Ray, he was the center of my existence. Now, that was all confused. So confused. And I did not understand all about Ray—why he did the things he did, things my daddy never did.

I was unusually quiet with daddy's return. I felt awkward. Mother was there too. That was difficult too. I watched her, wondering what to do. Since Ray's departure and our subsequent visit to Tulsa Bay, mother's visit with Ray without me, and my fall down the stairs at grandmother's, there had been a distance I had not experienced before.

Mother was more quiet and pensive. She would ignore me for long periods of time. It was very quiet in the house. She said she hoped that we would have tenants again soon to fill the front room. Tenants? But Ray wasn't a tenant, was he? Were tenants all like Ray?

Tenants did come. Two of them, like mother and daddy. And he did to her, like daddy to mother, like Ray to mother, like Ray to me. I was confused. The new tenant was so like Ray.

He too wore a uniform, but he was not like Ray. He ignored me. He ignored mother. I was confused. Angry almost. And why was he not like Ray? And why was Ray not like him?

I was so angry and confused. He made a joke with me one day. That scared me. I knew that making a joke with Ray had cost me dearly, had hurt and had made things happen. I did not understand. So I hit him. I hit him hard. He was so surprised he ran, trying to avoid being hit, calling for help. They did not stay for long, only a short while, it seems.

Daddy came home in the spring. There was so much emotion. Trying to please him. Not knowing how. We were, strangely, at odds with each other. I became afraid of him. This was new. Why didn't he treat me like he had before going to the service? Mother didn't help. She would talk to him about me, making it more difficult.

All the things that happened to me with Ray were blamed on me, not Ray

It seemed to reach him.

They were absorbed elsewhere, elsewhere, without me. It was not the same as before. I tried to get his attention and her attention. But it was not like before, and I felt more and more isolated. I began to act out more and more. Response was there, but it was not what was expected. It did not make things okay. It made things mad—mad at me, mostly. Punishment.

Daddy was angry, a lot. It hurt. I wanted my daddy back. I traded the doll he gave me for Christmas to a friend for her rag doll. I didn't want a doll from him. I wasn't his doll anymore! He was very put out by that. I didn't care. I did care.

Then daddy became all excited one day. He put me on his knee and spoke with me and teased with me, the old way, the way I missed. "How would you like to go to the circus? The circus is coming to town. It will be here real soon."

Daddy said that he had gone to the circus with his little sister when he was a child.

"Now, your mother's going to have to get busy, if there is to be a little sister or brother for you to take to the circus. I love the fun and excitement."

The circus had been an even bigger event back then than it was today, daddy explained.

They had elephants, lions, and tigers.

They had men and women walking on air and horseback riders, who stood on the horses' backs and flipped into the air.

"Let's see you do a somersault. Come on, you can do one, by just flipping off my lap. There!"

But I didn't want to leave his lap. I was entranced and excited and happy and relieved. My daddy was home. I was most excited for the upcoming visit to the circus, and so was daddy.

He took a bus all the way across town just to see what was going on. He talked on and on, about his experiences as a child at the circus. He seemed to be in another world. He was so, so energized. It was fun. And I could tease and play with him again. The day of the circus was soon to arrive.

Mother was okay too, I guess. But she was not to come with us. That was okay too, I guess.

*****

I was confused early at the circus. The trauma later that day would take precedence over the actual experience of the circus. And the pain of disbelief, anger, and separation were soon forgotten, too, or at least buried, beyond the events to transpire, shortly after the visit to the circus.

There was so much emotion and pain, so much horror, which was almost incomprehensible.

It is difficult to begin. Although begin I must. It would be important, much, much later on. It was a pivotal point, which lay hidden for many years. It was one of the last memories to come, and when it did, it came with great horror and fear, as if it had only just occurred. Indeed, it seemed to have just occurred when the recall began, catalyzed by the simple repetition of a key phrase from daddy: "I just don't understand you. I never have."

Chapter 6

My first recollection of the circus was the sound of a barking dog. As we approached the tents, I could hear a dog barking, yapping really, and someone yelling, "Shut that yapping dog up!"

At first, I was surprised by this discordant note on this day of anticipation and excitement. Then, however, as we walked around on the wet and trampled grasses, there was a peaceful quietness. The excitement was elsewhere.

We walked from wagon to wagon. First, we saw a mangy old lion and then a tiger, moving about restlessly in its wagon cage. Daddy said these were just to get the flavor, not the ones we would see perform.

Then we came to the tent where the elephants were tethered. The man with them was most congenial and let me touch them. A shudder ran through my body as I touched the rough, wrinkly skin of the elephant's face.

"A young one still," the old man said. "Wait until the elephant gets big—then no petting."

Daddy spoke with the man for a moment as I stared in disbelief at the elephant's face, eye, and trunk. I was puzzled and puzzled. I could not see much else of the elephant. There was not much elsewhere, except the big ears, yet a shudder ran through me.

I looked at the feet and the straw and the water bucket, absorbed in my thoughts.

"You better get that young lady to her seat. She looks kind of funny."

"It's probably all the excitement and strangeness."

Strangeness indeed.

We walked gingerly toward what seemed to be a path into the biggest tent. There were puddles of mud everywhere. The tent was enormous. I grabbed daddy's hand tightly as he fumbled through his pockets, looking for the tickets. From the sound of music, something was happening inside the tent, but I couldn't really see.

The clown man took the tickets and pointed way up the side to our seats. This wasn't good. What if I had to go to the bathroom? And where? Did they have houses for that? Daddy was not in the mood. I was to hold it!

This was a totally new world, way up high, on huge boards for walking and for sitting, with nothing under us. It was a huge place within the tent, really three tents, and things were happening everywhere. There was noise and loud music and people yelling and talking and eating strange stuff, as if they weren't suspended up on these boards, in the middle of nowhere. Emotions. People were yelling and screaming. Someone down below was yelling at the audience.

"The ringmaster," daddy said. "He's in charge. Watch him."

My mind was with the elephant, the elephant skin. I shuddered.

The ringmaster was making an announcement. "Ladies and gentlemen, the circus is about to begin. We ask your attention and your silence. The feat you are about to see ..."

All of the sudden, people in tight costumes were prancing around behind the ringmaster and grabbing huge ropes, suspended in the air, twirling them around and around, as one by one, the group of tightly clad people, worked their way up the ropes. All the while, others in the group were twirling the ropes in wide swings, and occasionally, the climbers would stop with their legs clutching the ropes, holding their arms out to the applause of the audience.

Suddenly, the climbing stopped, as the group, one by one, stepped on some sort of platform, high above the ring the ringmaster stood in. Then the real excitement began. Above the platforms were ropes with bars attached like swings. Daddy called it a trapeze. They dropped these, and pushed them back and forth, back and forth. Then one person on each platform grabbed a swinging bar, stopping the movement quite suddenly. Music or noise from below cut the silence. There was a beating of a drum. Then the two holding the bars leaped off the platform into the air. The force of their jump pushed the bar, and they began swinging, back and forth, back and forth, before jumping up and backward and turning around in midair to land on the tiny platforms again, while the others made room for them.

Once again, applause thundered as the two held their arms out to the crowd while leaning on their ropes. Then, just as suddenly, one jumped and was swinging again. And just as suddenly still, there were two people on the other swing, coming across and back and forth. The drum started up again as one of the swingers hung by his knees on the bar and reached out toward the other, swinging as he passed by. Then one jumped off the swing, somersaulted in midair and was caught by the hands of the upside down swinger. The crowd was silent, holding still, as if to help.

The two, opened their arms, while leaning on the ropes. The crowd went wild with applause. By now, all the seats around us were filled, and there was no way out of there, but down. It gave me a shudder, even to look down as a piece of paper fluttered down slowly to the ground.

Chapter 7

The circus sounds droned on as my mind wandered back to the elephant, his trunk, his deeply wrinkled skin.

Yes, it was like the skin around Ray's penis. I had acquired the word by asking a same-age male cousin.

When it had first happened and Ray had forced his thing in my mouth, all I could see was the skin, the wrinkly skin nearby, the strangely discolored skin nearby. The entire experience had been so shocking. I drifted away, away from where I was, away. Now, the feelings and memories pressed at me as a shudder. I could think of nothing else but the elephant skin.

Once I mentioned to daddy that the elephant reminded me of Ray, daddy grew quite silent—distant, silent, abrupt. I could feel it. It was a cold wall I could almost touch. He would start to talk about the circus and look at me in a loving manner. Then that sense of disturbance would come on, making the circus more poignant. The excitement, the parades went on and on, and the silence grew.

It stayed that way as we left the circus, the grass once wet, now dry and more trampled on. Daddy was pulling at me impatiently. On the bus home, we had to stand awhile and sat, finally. I looked out the window, distracted. Daddy was trying to straighten me out, to make me sit properly.

My mind would drift again. I knew something was wrong. Finally, I just sat staring at my black, patent leather shoes and the bits of grass stuck on them.

My feet were straight out in front of me. They don't make bus seats for little girls who have to sit straight back as their daddy tells them.

Mother was home when we got there. Daddy still had hold of my hand tightly. He swung me around and onto a dining room chair, my feet dangling.

"We have to talk. Mother, you back me. Maria Dee said something wicked and evil today. She likened the elephant's trunk unto Ray Owen's private part."

Daddy wouldn't use the word.

"This is totally unacceptable, young lady."

Mother became alert. I could feel her stinging stare.

"But it's true. It did. It did. It did," I started crying.

This seemed to anger daddy all the more, and I felt he was about to slap me.

"Young lady, we are going to wash your mouth out with soap. And you are never to use that word again, do you hear me?"

"But it's true. It's true.

"You don't love me. You hate me. I'm telling the truth, and you don't believe me!"

"I'll have no more of this. You are an evil, wicked child, and I never understand you!"

With that, he got up, slammed the door, and walked away from the house. I was devastated. I wanted to go to my room and cry. But my new little brother was in there sleeping, so mother forbade it.

Mother sent me outside with the admonishment that daddy was right, that I was never to say such things again.

"But."

"You heard me, never again, or you'll have much more to fear than getting your mouth washed out with soap. Now get out of here and think about what I said. And don't slam the screen when you go out."

I went outside, sitting first on the steps and then feeling too close and too warm and disturbed. I looked next door, but the neighbor's car was gone, and the screen was locked. So I went down in the shade of the two trees just beyond the Mac Corey's house, two doors away. They, the Mac Corey's, had daughters and yelled a lot, but it wasn't like that until now in our house.

I sat down on the concrete sidewalk, where there were still markers from playing hopscotch from the day before and, sort of, moved the rocks around on the ground. I was still in my Sunday dress and pinafore.

Daddy had selected it for me to wear to the big event, the circus. Some big event—it had just gotten me into trouble. I didn't understand. I had told the truth. It was what I had seen. It was what it looked like.

Daddy had looked so strange. He had been so angry. I couldn't remember that from him before. Before, I was always his little darling, his little angel. Mother was his big darling. I was his little darling. I always thought being little darling was better. What was I going to do now? *He left the house. He ran away. I love my daddy. I want him back.*

Tears ran down my cheeks and were about to drop on my good dress and pinafore. I wiped them as they reached my cheeks, smearing dirt from the rocks as I did along my cheeks. I must have been a sight, sitting spread eagle on the concrete, head down and crying, dirt smears on my face and clutching rocks all the while.

Suddenly, there was a shadow over me and big, bare feet at my side.

"Here, here now. It can't be all that bad." The man standing there offered me a hankie. Daddy was always playing hankie tricks.

"Here, here, let's get off the cold concrete. You'll catch cold." He knelt down beside me and took my chin and tilted my head upward.

"Now, now, what's so terrible that you're crying so about it? Tell me. Maybe I can help."

"I don't know."

"Now, now, what can it hurt?"

I blurted out, sobbing all the while, "My daddy just came home. Now he's gone away".

"Why?"

"Because, he's mad at me. He says I'm bad, very bad."

"Were you bad?"

"No. No. I told the truth."

"The truth?"

"Yes. I said what I saw."

"And what did you see?"

"The elephant and his big trunk."

"Oh, and, that made him mad?"

"What I said it looked like, and it did."

"Oh," he seemed to be amused, knowing. "Well, young lady, I know your dad, and he won't stay mad at you.

"Why don't you come with me, and I'll see what I can do to help."

Reluctantly, I followed him up the walk to his door.

Chapter 8

I'm here again. I don't know for how long. Amusing. Ice breaking. This exercise seems to frighten me, as does any exercise that might lead to being noticed myself. The dangers are many; the reasons abound.

"Why?"

"Why, indeed."

"Because you know and in knowing, you must die."

That's what he said. Those were his very words. They could have been the words of others also. Those could have been the words of others who, because I knew, felt threatened, others who have had that power over me. And yet, I escaped, and more than once. And I escaped in more than one manner.

What a mixed heritage. I had a brilliant mind. Yet I was fearful of knowledge, fearful that it would lead to discovery and, therefore, to death. I would like to say death of the old and discovery of the new. But these are not words spoken symbolically or figuratively.

Because of knowledge, my life, this life, was repeatedly put in danger. Through lack of knowledge, my life was defended, I survived. But how did I survive? I was fearful of discovery, sabotaging that which might lead to discovery. And my own thirst for knowledge and curiosity led me to these dangers so were not to be trusted either. I felt paralyzed either way. I was trapped by the fear of the danger of discovery, of learning. I was trapped by the fear that any doing might lead to discovery of me and that I had knowledge.

The confusion mounts. The labyrinth tightens. What was I to do? Avoid being discovered. Do not know too much. Be seen the fool. Will this disarm the enemy?

It didn't altogether, not really. But escape I did, at that time, although not without damage, further hindering me. Now able to understand, I am, still, hovering with fear—of discovery, of being discovered—and life is swiftly going away. I grit my teeth. They are being moved out of alignment from the constant pressure. The jaws ache from tension. Why do I hold on so tightly to my defense? Either pretending or poised to defend? Neither allows for my dreams, ambitions, or desire.

All say, "Don't. You will be discovered. You will be killed. You will be killed."

I accepted the man's offer to help. I walked up the steps to his house, where, he said, he would call and speak to daddy. He sat me on the couch and went to get me a drink of water. He came back with water, but something else too. It was big and seemed sharp, pointed. At first, I thought it was scissors. But, no, it was something else—something like a knife, but bigger, flatter.

Something snapped inside my brain, and I knew I was in great danger. He sensed it too as I backed away from the glass of water in his hand. He moved swiftly, now pinning me down against the arm of the couch. I could not move and was very afraid. Yet I did not cry out. I did not black out, as before with Ray.

I stayed there, in the scene, somehow sensing the danger and the need to be alert. I could not do anything about what was happening.

He opened his pants and pulled out his private part. He moved swiftly, determined, and not saying a thing. He pulled down my pants, took his fingers, pulling me apart, while pushing me against the couch. He pushed himself inside me. The pain was terrible. Yet I stayed. I did not float away to other places. I stayed. I watched, emotionless and motionlessly, as he pushed at me. Tears running down my face, I gritted my teeth at the pain, at the fear.

With his part inside me, he picked me up, holding my body to him and began jerking me, violently, around the room.

I clung to him in fear, gripping his shoulders with my nails, as he tried to beat my back and head into the wall. *This is too much. How can I bear it?*

My head is beginning to bleed, where it hit the wall. I am scared, frightened, and yet I fight not to leave, not to blank out, like I always did before with Ray.

He is moving back toward the couch. He throws me down again, against the arm of the couch as he pulls out of me. Then pins my left shoulder down with his knee, almost cutting my breath away, and penetrates my mouth, with his part spewing stuff into my mouth.

I gag. Then I bite. He quickly pulls back in anger and grabs the instrument he had brought from the kitchen.

I yell out, "Why?"

He responds, "Because you know, and in knowing, you die."

That's what he said. Those were his very words. They could have been the words of others also.

Others who, because I knew, felt threatened, others who have had that power over me. And yet, I escaped mentally, and more than once.

I kicked at him, causing him to lose his grip on the knife object. It flipped through the air.

Somehow, I grabbed it with my free hand, my right hand, and started bringing it, up and down, in quick, repeated strokes.

I could not stop. I was petrified to stop—that I would be killed if I stopped. I hit, again and again and again, until I could not move.

I remember at one point the shocked look in his eyes, and then later he seemed to grab at my hand as I dropped my arm, holding it stiffly out from me.

I felt his energy leave as he grasped at my arm. I was still there, pinned against the couch by his body, with the knife object hanging from my hand—just staring, unable to move, when the lady came and found me there.

"Oh, you poor, dear child," she said as she pried the instrument from my hand.

Chapter 9

I ask myself, where am I?

Back here, on the page. Can I write? Why must I write? The day does not answer, and yet I write. My soul, it writes. How do I tell my soul that it is for it that I write?

The deed's done. The event's told. The experience was remembered, relived. It's there. That's all. That's all?

How I wish that it was not at all—that what happened was not at all.

My body spoke, well before the mind would let it out. Too horrible, too frightening, the experience is something my mind can't bear. I don't want to encounter the experience. Yet at night or in the quiet of day, abruptly, flashes—horrible, uninvited flashes—occur.

Fear takes over, and I fight to stop the flashes. I call out. I wait. I want support. I will not walk that way again, alone. I was alone and then numb, unmoving, staring. The knife object still in my right hand, my body wedged between the lamp table, the couch, and the man. The man had reached out his hand to me, touching my arm with the knife object, just as he stopped and seemed to melt to the floor. I stood there. I don't know how long. I could do nothing.

The tears were now running down my cheeks; my body began to shake. What had happened? How had it come to this? Flashes of being swung about the room, the wanting to scream and scream and scream, yet, somehow, somehow enduring, watching, biting my lip, gritting my teeth, tensing my jaw, trying to mute my own screams and horror.

Why not scream? Why not cry for help? What help, where, and from whom? Who would help me? Mother? Not before. And she was too far away. And I was not supposed to be here, she'd say.

There's no one here to hear. And—quick—my mind is slipping. He's moving to the couch again. Oh, this is not good. He's too big. I can't move. Ugh, he's moving out of me and pinning me with his knee. I am in pain. I can't breathe from his weight. Help me. Help me. Dear God. Help me. I am overwhelmed.

What? His penis is in my mouth. Bite, bite. I try to bite. Yes, yes, yes. He's mad. He's swearing.

He's pulling back. Yes, yes, yes. He's grabbing the knife thing. I tell myself, *Keep kicking at him.* The knife thing—it's flying, flipping through the air. Grab it, grab it, grab it. Yes, yes, yes.

Hit. Hit. Hit. *Yes. Yes. Yes.* Keep hitting. Don't stop. Don't stop. Stay in the mind.

He's trying to stop you. He's trying to stop you. He's trying to stop you. He's grabbing for your arm. He's there in front of you, quiet. All the room is quiet. I can't hear him.

He's not moving. I can hear my own body screaming, screaming, screaming, sobbing and screaming.

The room is silent. Something inside me looks out at him, wanting to touch him, to touch his forehead, to know. It's as if, in the shock, I do not recognize what has happened. With a wave of emotion, I am immersed again in the horror, upon horror, which kept coming. I am trying to stay, to stay in the room, not to leave, to leave with the mind and go far away. I am scared, too scared to leave. I'm scared not to stay, to stay in the room.

Where am I? The mind goes blank. Where am I?

There is a sound. Someone is at the door. A woman calls hesitantly. "Harry, Harry. Is that you?"

I look down at the body crumpled on the floor.

"Harry? Is that you?"

I am sick in the stomach, overwhelmed by a feeling of nausea. New fears. What will happen now? I fixate on the body. I hear a click in the door, a crick of sound. The mind is racing, even while the body is immobile. I can't move. I can't leave. I can't do anything. I am scared. I don't know what to anticipate. What will happen? What will happen now?

I am overwhelmed. I am sobbing and sobbing and sobbing. The whole body is shaking now, with sobbing. I am screaming within. I can hear myself within. Yet outwardly, I can't seem to see, to feel. I am motionless.

She is touching me on my shoulder. A chill of recognition of where I am and what's happened runs through me. I am aware of the room. She's talking, saying something. I can't seem to hear her. I am only aware she's talking to me.

"Oh, you poor child."

I heard that. A shudder runs through me—the sense of it, *poor child*, in all its meaning. It is overwhelming to me in its overpowering sense of reality. No rebellion, just recognition. Poor child. It is an abysmal feeling, a feeling of abyss.

It is raining outside now as I write this. It is a gentle rain. I am filled with sadness, awareness. Oh, this writing is so painful. The pain and acknowledgment of the depth of that moment is all there. Poor child. Me.

Even in writing, the tears do not come. I am still there, numb, hearing the woman saying, "Oh, you poor child."

I want to cry out. I want to say, "No. It is not me!" Why me. Oh dear God, why me?

The time is slow. She takes my hand, my hand, immobile at my side, still clutching the knife thing. There is a pain in my forearm, a numbness of pain as the fingers are pulled, one by one, from the grip of the knife thing. As the muscles in the arm resist, I am immobile, with this object. I am a part of the object.

The body cries within. I am overwhelmed. I am not all there now. My mind is adrift; my mind is numb. I do not want to leave this scene. I'm suspended here, so to speak. Yet the sense of tears within is so strong.

Oh, dear God. Can I cry within, without crying without?

I do not want to be, to be this "poor child." And yet, how can I not be?

Thoughts of apricot jam on toasted muffin. Where was that? My mind searches for a pleasant memory.

I seek something to cause a smile, a positive thought.

The woman stepped over the body, to better reach me. It is awkward. I sense the juxtaposition of him and me. I feel almost frozen there in time. I sense that I am the child standing there, frozen in time, this poor child in a state of shock, at what the child has done, feeling tarnished, both by what she has done and by what he has done, and how isolated she was in coming here.

No protection by mother, no acceptance by daddy. Yet now, just now, this day, there is a sense of lifting, of being lifted, from the scene. The lack of protection, the no acceptance, the actions upon her she can feel.

The woman is lifting her out of the corner created by the lamp stand, the couch, and his body. She and the child sense what has happened to her body below, and also, what has been done by her arm and action. The memories are there and in the throat too, where she could not scream, and in the jaws, held tight, the biting jaws, the overwhelm of emotion in the cheeks and jaws.

After all the years and years and years, this has, seemingly, been dormant. Dormant, you say? All the times of being in that corner, caught between the lamp stand, the couch, and his body.

Even today, I escape bed early morning—escape during late-night sleeping hours from my bed and the corner between the standing lamp and the place where I lay in bed and my husband's sleeping body, escape the troubled sleep—and retreat to my favorite place downstairs, the place where I sit now writing, righting this.

No wonder, sometimes there is an unexplained aversion to staying in bed, the pretend corner upstairs, to escape to quiet and peace downstairs, until I feel restored, quieted once again. I want to scream.

There are an entire series of points of being "frozen," unable to move, to act, to scream, to speak. This is important. Each time is to be honored, so to speak, in order to move through it.

This memory was the last to come, after formal therapy had ended, after sequential events involving Ray had been told. This memory was in isolation from the others. Yet it was within the sequence and influenced the events to come.

Now, today, I can "see" the multiplicity of moments, one after another, of paralysis, now seen as inertia today. I can only hope and trust that I will fully move through each of these "breaks" to allow flow again within my soul.

Why do I say *my soul*? Because the lack of flow, the paralysis is deafening to me, to my soul. It rains gently again. I am trying. I am trying to stay here and with the scene long enough for a sense of flow to begin.

Chapter 10

Where am I? Teeth gnashing, tongue thrust against my teeth. Pain is emanating from the mouth and moving upward. The head is splitting with pain ...

Help, I want to cry. But I do not cry. I am numb, voiceless. Tears, where are they? Why won't they come? Why? Why? Why? Oh, to cry. I am lost. I don't know what to do.

I am frightened, scared to death. What do I do? What? How can I say this? He's so, so "unmoving."

Why? Why did he come at me? Why did he do those things? Why wasn't he— He said that he was a friend of daddy's, someone who could help? Why wasn't ...

I didn't want to do this. Why did he attack me? Yes, he said, "because of what you know."

Oh God, help me. I am so frightened. I am all the while, frozen within my body. I begin to shake.

Then I'm aware the woman is moving me somehow. I am so frightened and cold. She's fussing over my dress, wiping me and the dress with a cold, wet cloth.

"There, there. Dry your tears. It's going to be all right."

How will it be all right? What can I do? What have I done? Why? I am so scared. I want to cry. I want to cry.

She's washing me off. She thinks the dress will dry real soon. Then I must go home. Then I must stay away from here. Then I must not talk about this. Then I must not talk about this to anyone. Do I hear? She's putting me back together again, she says. I'll be as pretty as new. How? How?

Humpty Dumpty sat on a wall. Humpty Dumpty had a great fall. I am scared. Who is this lady? Why is she caring for me this way?

"Do you hear me? You must promise me you will not tell anyone. Anyone, do you hear? Do not tell anyone. You have never been in this place. Do you hear me?"

My hands are shaking. She takes them and wipes them off again with the wet cloth. I look downward. She tilts my head, with her hand on my chin and another on my shoulder.

She again says, "You poor, dear child. You must do as I tell you. It's important. We don't want any harm to come to you now, do we? Now, let me hear, 'Yes, ma'am.'"

"Yes, ma'am. No words are spoken for a time.

She looks at me, as if she might say more but has no words to say.

"It hurts. It hurts so much."

"What hurts?"

"My mouth. My mouth hurts."

"Is that all that hurts?"

I shake my head and lower my eyes. "No, ma'am."

But. I'm afraid to talk about it. I think, I've been punished in some strange way, so best not to talk about it. I sense flashbacks to the scenes before—being whirled around the room, my head being beaten against the wall, gritting my teeth, afraid to yell, wanting to "leave," the knife thing, the biting, and coming down on my own mouth, as he pulled away, his look of rage and anger, the knife thing flying through the air.

The woman seems to sense that I am drifting away. She starts to take me to the couch. Then she stops and indicates a big, stuffed chair, low to the ground. She straightens my dress. She checks my shoes. She looks up at me from where she's kneeling on the floor.

"You've been through quite a scare, I'm sure, by the looks of things. But you'll be all right. You'll be all right. I'm sorry. I'm sorry for you this happened. I'm sorry it happened here in my house. I'm sorry. I'm going to take care of it, so don't you worry your pretty little head about it, you hear? Now take a deep breath. That's right. And dry those tears."

What tears? I can't cry. Not now, not ever. It's all gone, all gone. Daddy doesn't love me, this has happened, all the other with mother. What am I to do?

There is an angel standing there. It seems to say, "Go home now, Maria, and be quiet. It is best."

The woman opens the door and looks out. The street is quiet.

"Now, run along home. And remember, it is best not to say anything about this."

I am out the door, and she closes it behind me. I sit on the steps awhile. I can feel her watching from inside. After a while, I move up the street to behind Mary's house and watch back down the street.

Sometime later, I see him being wheeled out on a stretcher bed, with neighbors standing around. There is some hushed whispering I can't hear. I look to see if Mary is there. She's watching from her porch. She sees me by her bushes and invites me in.

She shakes her head, saying, "A young un like you shouldn't be watching this."

She indicates that I should come inside and come to the kitchen with her.

"Let's sit you down and get some milk and cookies I baked for Jack. He'll never miss them."

She chuckles to herself.

"Well, what have you been up to this fine day?"

"I'd rather not say."

"Oh, I see," she said. "One of *those* days."

Dear God, this is so hard, so difficult. It overwhelms me at times. Oh, dear God, I must trust you to rescue me!

Chapter 11

Here again. Love. What is love? Where is love? Love is rain falling on leaves, on the ground where I sat before that man came to help me get my daddy back.

Well, it didn't happen that way. Daddy was home when I returned from Mary's.

"Where have you been, young lady? We've been worried sick about you."

"I was helping Mary."

"Oh, well, all right. But next time, you must get permission before you go out. Your mother and I have had a little talk about your comment about Ray, and I don't know where you got that word. But it is not 'ladylike' to use that word or to speak of a man's private parts. Do you hear me?"

"Yes, sir"

"What?"

"Yes, daddy."

"That's better. Now tell me you're going to be a good girl and mind your mother. She tells me you have been quite difficult of late, and I won't tolerate it. Do you hear me?"

"Yes, sir."

"What!"

"Yes, daddy."

"Now run to the bathroom and clean up; it's just about time for supper. And, Maria Dee, your mother reminds me. Stay away from the houses at the end of the block. I don't know what happened down there today, but it was something bad, and I don't want you hanging around there. You have enough friends, right here in the middle of the block."

"What happened down there?"

"I don't know. It looks like a man was killed, in some sort of fight. Cut up real bad, they say. It's not the kind of thing for little girls to hear about."

"Daddy?"

"Yes?"

"I was there. I did it to the man."

"Maria Dee."

"Chris, this is just what I'm talking about."

"Maria, I will have no more of this lying. Even if you were there, you shouldn't have been. Do you hear me? Now, go to your room. You don't need supper tonight. I want you to think about what you've said. Telling a lie is a sin, do you hear me?"

"I wasn't telling a lie. I wasn't supposed to tell, but I wasn't telling a lie."

"What do you mean, you weren't supposed to tell?"

"The lady said so."

"What lady?"

"The lady down the street."

"So, you were down the street. You know that's off limits. Now, go to your room immediately. There will be no more discussions, no more lies out of you tonight, young lady."

"Yes, daddy."

"That's a good girl. Now, give your mother a good night kiss and go to bed and close the door."

I looked at the table set for dinner. He noticed.

"No dinner, remember."

"Perhaps, I could bring her something later?"

He frowns, looking at Frances. "Well, maybe."

After the door shuts, there is a long silence as they begin supper.

"Do you think she was telling the truth?"

"Goodness, Frances, the man was brutally attacked. This is no child's handiwork. Maria Dee has no sense of reality. For her to fanaticize this—that she did this terrible act—where is she coming from? I just don't understand. I never have!"

"Well, she does spend a lot of time alone or talking with the older women in the neighborhood. She does have some pals in the neighborhood, but maybe they're not good for her. The neighborhood seems rough, you know. Things have changed since we first moved here."

Silence.

"Maybe. I was thinking—I was talking with Merle—that I'd start up a Blue Bird group. There would be new friends for Maria to play with, and it would give her some structure too."

"Maybe. We'll see. I'll think about it. I don't want you to work too hard. You need to take care of yourself. You're my sweetheart, right?"

"Yes, but, this wouldn't be a problem. I've done it before."

"Yes, but that was before you were married and had other responsibilities."

He smiles shyly at her and makes a move toward her, to give her a hug and a kiss.

There is a great reticence on her part. His mind wanders to Maria Dee, and he places the blame for this squarely on her misbehavior. He pulls back his chair, and starts clearing the table.

Frances protests, but he says, "It's okay." He doesn't mind helping.

"Let Maria alone. One night without dinner won't hurt, and it will give her something to think about."

Thinking, indeed. Maria Dee cried, quietly, for quite a while at this latest rejection by her father. Why was it so? Why was he like this? There had been so much hope—that his return would, somehow, make everything right. Was that ever to be?

I don't know, she said, almost out loud. Her thoughts focused on this, too afraid to think back on the events of the day, too afraid of the punishment. She was afraid to think.

Chapter 12

Where are you, sweet Maria?
Crying was heard in the ethereal.
Where are you, sweet Maria?
Angels cry for you, sweet Maria.
Ease your pain. Let the tears remain.
They will not stain away the pain.

Where are you, sweet Maria?
Unable to bear the pain, are you?
Here's some bile from my wounds to bear the pain.
Here's some vinegar from my lips to anesthetize
the pain.
Here are my angels, to wash away the pain.

***

I saw an angel once when clouds were passing by ...
   Mother said a bluebird perched upon my windowsill once when
I was ill.
   I don't know.
   I saw an angel once when clouds were passing by ...
   The angel picked her up and carried her ever so gently up into
the first layer of clouds, to help her rest, to heal from all that had

transpired that day. It was too much for her to bear all by herself. That's how it came to be that Maria spent the night among the angels alight on the first layer of clouds, just safe enough from the cares of the day. Safe, safe for the stay. Washed in the gentleness of angels' songs, she drifted into sweet forgetfulness of that day. All that remained as a memento of the day was a rage and anger at seeming injustice done to anyone.

Left too was a desire to sleep peacefully once more, bathed by angels' songs in soft moonlight.

It was the next autumn after daddy had returned from the war. They took a journey west to visit daddy's best friend and mother's girlfriend and their two daughters, who surrounded Maria in age. The journey was a blur—driving all night, an exciting place with little airplanes, and a public eating place.

It was mother's friend's new home, much as ours had been for us when mother had first wanted to go away. It was a place that seemed less than friendly for mother's friend too, and she shared her tears with mother.

But she was different from mother. She spoke oh so lovingly of her girls, her creativity, and her love. She was happy, unhappy there—unlike mother, who was just unhappy at home.

Maria's heart jumped as, suddenly, she was picked up in the air, swung around, off the ground, like an airplane circling would do. Her daddy and his friend laughed at the fun of seeing her fly by, as if an airplane. Holding her legs stiff and moving her round and round through the air—was it? Yes, it was Ray. He was not in uniform, as before. How did he get here? Was he everywhere? A lot had happened since Ray, and she had daddy with her now.

Yet mother seemed apprehensive, as she yelled, "Put her down. You'll make her sick!"

Sick indeed. Since the moment Maria had realized just who was swinging her, she had been sick all over. Why? Why was he here?

Chapter 13

"Blessings on your journey, sweet child."

Dear, sweet child—Mother's friend, Carol, called me that, even with having two children. It made me feel special. I was aglow. I was happy. There was much fun and kidding and laughter.

Ray was there. Much emotion. Could I tell him what had happened? No, I thought not. It all seemed so vague now anyway.

Carol's house was so cheery, so fun, so warm and friendly. I wanted the same for us. Carol did come to visit us and painted our table along with aunt Dorothy, who was also visiting. They were both professional artists. The kitchen held the memory of her and her cheerfulness.

Ray was daddy's best friend's brother. So daddy knew Ray too. This was most puzzling. Why was he here? He wasn't necessary. Daddy had mother. His brother had Carol. Why was Ray here?

It was difficult to think with Ray there. I went back into the house, the screen door slamming.

Carol responded, "You mustn't do that. Gentle, Maria—close the screen gently. Otherwise it won't last."

"Carol doesn't look well."

"She'll be all right. It's probably Ray's airplane ride."

"You should leave the piloting to your brother. That's his profession."

I sat there on the couch wondering what to do next. The girls were at school, so I couldn't hide with them. Why was he here? I didn't want him to be here. What if daddy found out about him and about mother? I had already figured out I couldn't tell daddy about Ray, not anymore, not after what had happened.

Not after all that. I didn't want daddy to get mad at me again. "No way, Jose," as daddy's friend would say.

Time moves slowly sometimes. Scenes hurt to remember. Some I'm less willing to tell; I sense more shame in this remembering. Ray used me. He used me. He abused me. There is pain in the telling.

I was restless at dinner that night. Ray and the girls and I were alone. Mother, daddy, and the girls' parents were gone somewhere together for the night. Out on the town, they said. Ray volunteered to take care of us girls.

Rooster crowing. That's what Ray was doing—he was making like a rooster crowing. There were pictures of chickens and roosters painted on the walls, and there was a play rooster on the table.

"Cock-a-doodle-do. Cock-a-doodle-do. Do I do. Cock-a-doodle-do."

The girls seemed quiet. They seemed apprehensive too. Lynn, the big one and the tough one, did not like being ordered around by Ray. There is so much to remember.

Chapter 14

Ray was always the prankster, the joke player, the game player. He had a game for us all that night. It was a beautiful, clear, starry night. We were on the desert. That's what they called this strange earth. It had a very different look from home. The night was dark, yet bright. The stars were endless in the sky, stretching on and on.

It was very quiet where we were. There was only the sound of a radio in the background. The radio was in the kitchen near the window. The lights from the house cast plenty of light as we crossed the yard. The rooster, Ray, led us, chickens, across the yard to the playhouse. Lynn and Diana's mama had painted the room in bright colors and put small chairs, a table, and a bench, where we, the small ones as she called us, could play. I think the room must have been for chickens; it was so small.

Ray looked silly and big entering the place where we, the small ones, could play. He sang a little song about the crows. He danced about, and we were to follow. Diana was interested. Lynn was not. I was not sure. Diana giggled. Ray had tickled her. Tickled her fancy, he said. She was very squirmy, suddenly. Ray had arranged us in the room. Diana was on the bench with him, Lynn was on the chair beside him, and I was at the table. He closed the door. We were getting ready to play his little game, he said.

"Hey, Doc. Hi, Dee. Hi, diddle Dee." We three. What he could mean, we could not know.

The memory of that starry evening in the playroom with Ray is all faded now. We were to be a play, for him to teach us. What was he to teach us? We gathered together, round and round the room, as chickens, he said, before he sat us down—Lynn on the chair, Diana on the bench beside him, me near the table. We were all beside him. It was not a tall room.

"When are the grown-ups coming back?" I asked.

"Not tonight, not tonight."

Oh. So that was it. He had us alone. The awareness really began to set in. He suddenly closed the door.

"I don't want to stay in the room."

"Ooh, yes, you do," he said, suddenly setting me on the table.

"And you're going to be the lead chicken tonight, to show the others the rooster's delight."

With this, he kneeled at the table on one knee and slightly on the chair I had been sitting on, before he lifted me onto the table.

"Spread your legs apart so that we can show the others the chicken and rooster in the light."

I tried to back off the table, but this did not help, as it caused me to lose my balance. He grabbed me by the legs as I started to fall off the table and toward the bench. Diana moved along the bench, and Lynn started to stand up. Ray reached out and pushed Lynn down on the chair.

"Don't you do that. Nobody is leaving here."

There was tension in the room. I was sick and worried and wanted to wet my pants. I had wet my pants and mother's dress on the train when we brought daddy home from the war. There were so many soldiers there on the train everywhere—wearing uniforms everywhere.

I began to fade out, with the memory of what Ray had done to me and of the men on the train.

I could feel Ray touching me, suddenly. Touching me. I kept fading out. He kept saying something about chickens and roosters. Why was he doing this to me?

I got in trouble on the train, when I wet on mother. She shook me and ran me to the train room. She was really upset.

My mind wandered, afraid to come back to the playroom. Why was he touching me? Why? I did not know what to do. He kept pushing at me, talking rooster talk. Why wouldn't he leave me alone? I was afraid to remember the rest of the scene.

He threatened us, all three of us—that he would punish us if we told. It was a chicken and rooster game, he said, just a chicken and rooster game; no harm done. He made us each promise not to tell before we were let out of the playroom.

I was afraid he would tell that Maria had wet her pants in the playroom.

*****

He came back to see us in Texas, when my new brother came home from the adoption agency, where mother had worked. My new brother was not a baby but almost ready to learn to walk.

Something I taught him right away.

Ray's return visit caused mother to be upset, very upset. She was very upset with Ray.

She said, "You have betrayed me."

With Ray came my aunt Kim. It was difficult to see this—Ray, who I knew; my aunt Kim, who I knew; now, she says, they are married. There is a strange emptiness inside me. Mother too. Mother takes my hand and moves me toward the house.

"Go, show your aunt your new baby brother. She'll love him as much as you do."

Aunt Kim and I entered the bedroom. Sonny was sleeping. She picked him up and rocked him back and forth, back and forth, talking funny talk to him and holding him up to look at him. I slipped out of the room, down the hall, to the front bedroom, where I could see Ray and mother talking. Ray was holding mother at the shoulders, mother pushing him away at the chest.

"Frances, listen to me. You know it wouldn't work. We both know it. Kim is sweet, warm, and loving, and she loves me."

"It's so sudden. You didn't tell me."

"How?"

"You've betrayed me, left me abandoned to this. You promised."

"I know, what I said. But I couldn't. I couldn't break up the marriage. This way, we'll all be one, happy family—Maria Dee, you, and me."

Maria Dee, you, and me. So now there were three—Kim, mother, and me.

Chapter 15

Christmastime was always special and exiting for me.

With cousins and aunts and uncles on both sides of the family, Christmas was a time of gifts, gifts, hum. Gifts.

The gifts of that Christmas—where were the gifts of that Christmas?

We traveled from Texas to California that Christmas, with a stop in Arizona. That was where Ray was. That was where his family was. That was where Kim had moved when she'd married Ray.

That was where her new baby boy was. That was where my world came apart. That was where my story came apart. During that trip, that was where I lost my heart.

During that trip, that was where I was pulled apart. Bits of me were left scattered along the desert ridges. Bits of my mind were scattered here and there. That was where my heart finally closed down, accepting imprisonment within the stone cold existence of mother's heart.

Mother is old now and ridden with memory loss, oddly appropriate—after I'd given her my mind to control so many years ago. It would be her mind to go, now that my memories are returning and my heart is experiencing its own definition.

It was a horrific Christmas trip in recall. Yet for years, the definition of joy and happiness seemed to be contained in writing, "Merry Christmas."

That was how strong the effort was not to remember. My poor mind, what it must have suffered, as I surrendered to Ray's threat of death, if I did not forget. By then, I had come to believe that I must forget in order to survive. It was a strange struggle of splitting apart, in order to remain.

The emotion wells up in me at the very thought of how this had to be.

Chapter 16

Archangel Michael guards the Northern Gate,
guiding us home to the heart of love.
—Pocketful of Miracles

Archangel Michael descended over me, protecting me with his very being as I took that abrupt and shocking journey back through time.

In the process now, I can sense the suddenness of departure, as she angrily struck two fingers within me again and again, with her shouting, "I'll show you what it's like. I'll show you what it's like."

Her anger and refusal to accept the truth of Maria's plight—why she had found Maria wandering and crying outside the house, why Ray had said to her, "You'd better look to Maria. She's struck her head, and she's all upset."

Maria, it was known by all by now, was wildly imaginative. Ray had said so. Ray had pronounced it some time ago to the belief of all adults.

"The child's a born liar, with a very vindictive bent. She is not to be trusted. Not to be trusted. Her imagination and fantasies run wild." That's what he had said.

Maria's mother had filled Maria's head full of stories and fairies—like the poem of sugar plum fairies, dancing in her head.

Maria's mother had more to dread. Her own behavior might be told by Maria, and in the saying, her marriage might be dead.

Her mother stabbed Maria, again and again, in the vagina with her fingers held together.

"She'll know now what she has said."

I feel numb today. Why this feeling of dread, what have I said, that she wishes me dead. I lie upon my bed. I am filled with fear and dread. I am tired. The mind will not compute. Why this feeling of dread. Why this feeling of wanting to be dead? I can't speak with the mommy that I know. She did something to me. I know, I dread, even wishing I were dead. Waves wash over me. Am I soothed? No. I am feeling dead.

Where am I? Who am I? I am dead. I feel blank. There's something, someone, outside of me, wishing me dead.

My realities are so different from that then. It wasn't until my psychotherapist that I slipped back in, released, so to speak, from the fear of fire within.

When mother gouged me repeatedly, my very soul within responded in flight. The flight was too swift from within, evoking a departure to somewhere within, a place filled with incense and humming and with burning and screaming within. It was a place of torture and pleading, of bleeding within.

It was not until the recall that I saw Michael the Archangel there, over me and protecting me as I made that horrific journey within—within to a place of caves and caverns, lit by candles and flames from within. The angst of my blood ran hot as the flames leaped at my heart and the smoke and cinders burned my eyes.

Through the flames from my pyre, I see her standing there in the shadow, in the shade. Safely away from the flames, she stares at me, just stares, as my heart is torn out by the flames.

Dear God. "Why?" I cry. Dear God. "Why?" I cry. As I know, I die as the flames reach toward the sky. The horror is so strange. The pain. Why? Death came with overwhelming pain.

I awoke the next day, strangely detached in feeling. I hate this feeling of not knowing where I am, why I am here, why I sense there is something to fear. This will not be easy, this remembering.

Lord, be with me. Keep me, dear Lord. Keep me.

Chapter 17

Sadness. Music. What do I know of these? Indian music.

"We're going to visit Ray's mom and dad today. They have a farm, a tree farm. We're going to get some oranges from their tree farm."

"No. It's a grove. That's what Ray said. Not a tree farm."

"Uncle Ray to you."

"He's not my uncle."

"He's your uncle since he married your aunt Kim."

"Why did he do that?"

"What?"

"Marry aunt Kim?"

"I suppose because he loves her."

"Did he have to get married?"

"Maria Dee, that's no question for a young lady to ask!"

"Why not?"

"Now, don't smart answer me. Sit there and be quiet. Enough of your questions."

"Yes, Ma'am."

"Don't 'yes ma'am' to me. What do you say, young lady?"

"Yes, mother."

"That's better."

"But is it? Who said so?"

Maria Dee is always the argumentative one. She'll be a lawyer for sure.

"Maria Dee, sit still, and leave your brother alone."

"I wasn't doing anything."

"Don't say that to me, young lady. You sit by your window and leave your brother be."

"I'm tired, mother. I want to go home."

"No, Maria Dee. You are not tired. You are just being naughty. Now, sit still and be quiet."

My head against the window, I watched as we drove through plots of land with white fences and trees with oranges and lemons and little houses with no yards, just trees. It was the first time I can remember seeing oranges and lemons on trees that way. They were big trees but not as tall as the nut tree at home.

I felt tired and bored. I didn't like this grown-up visit thing. You couldn't do anything right, and Sonny was off limits for playing with. Ray had seen to that. He'd gotten me in trouble. He said that I did bad things to my brother. It wasn't so. But they were all really mad at me. And I felt at such a loss. They were yelling and screaming at me, but I couldn't remember what happened—only that Ray had said I was a very bad girl and mother had chimed in too. Then daddy got really mad. This trip was what was really bad. And I can't remember why; I suddenly felt that I had been away somewhere. I was screaming and could hardly get my breath when I came back.

Ray had told them that he had found me with my mouth on Sonny's private part and had given me a spanking right then and there.

I responded, "No, no, no. I didn't! No, no!"

"Maria Dee!"

Daddy had a very strong grip on me. I struggled to get loose. He only tightened his grip. I was afraid to look at him; he was so angry with me.

"Look at me! This instance, do you hear me!"

"Yes, sir."

Tears streamed down my cheeks. I was beginning to feel sick in the stomach. *Dear God, this is painful.* Mother once said, "Think on the beautiful things." I did. I do. It helps. It soothes.

"Maria Dee. You lied to us and hurt your little brother. This is a very bad, bad thing. You are a wicked, sinful child."

I am feeling overwhelmed by his yelling yet afraid to remember and in pain where Ray hurt me. I had come into the room where Sonny was kept and saw Ray touching Sonny. It made me very angry. Ray was playing with Sonny the way he had played with me, except that Sonny was smaller and different down there than me.

I started beating on Ray's back, trying to make him stop. That seemed to make Ray very angry. He whipped around and threw me down on the floor, where he had been playing with Sonny. He grabbed me by the back of the neck and shoulders and forced me down, almost so my face was touching Sonny's tummy. I struggled to move my head, but his grip was strong.

Then he grabbed Sonny's private part with one hand, and pushed my face down on it, while trying to force my mouth open. I gritted my teeth.

He kept pressuring me and yelling for me to open my mouth. He forced me further down on Sonny, my teeth touching Sonny's part. I was repulsed. Then it seemed unreal.

Suddenly, he was doing something behind me. I could hear he was unbuckling his belt and pants. I could feel him against my leg. I tried to cry out, but would not open my mouth. He was so strong. He was moving my panties. *What is he doing? This is not right.* The pain in my rear was excruciating.

I did not know how long I'd been there, lying on the floor next to Sonny crying. I only knew my rear hurt inside and that Ray was shouting and hitting at me. I cringed. I could see teeth marks on Sonny. I cried and cried and cried. I could not understand what had happened—why I hurt so; why Ray was hitting me; why the adults came running at his call; why daddy picked me up and shook me;

why mother kept trying to tell him to calm down, that he'd kill me if he weren't careful.

But I couldn't understand. I felt like I had awakened to a nightmare. Where had I been? What happened? How could I have hurt Sonny? And why did I hurt so inside?

"I can't protect you." I have a memory of this phrase, of knowing I couldn't protect Sonny when Ray first returned with Kim and Sonny had just arrived from the adoption agency.

Chapter 18

The call to write is strong. I know not why or about what exactly. The story continues. I am sad. I am forlorn. I am lost. Though, as I write this, I am not. I am in that place and that time.

And that place *and* time continues with me at some level. I am here. I am there. The commitment is to bring me home. Home. Where is home? The saying, home is where the heart is, need not apply. In this, it is not so. Or is it too much so? Dichotomy. Yin and yang. I don't know. I know. I write and I write to bring me home.

There was much, much more to happen before they would bring me home that year—or, at least, bring what was left of me home. I truly died out there in the desert, before they brought me home. Many memories flow through my head at once. Which shall I tell next? Which will come next? The mind is, perhaps, very deliberate and aware. That me I know little of is deliberate and aware—that mind that left that day, not to even attempt to return for many a year.

For many a year, there were only glimpses/memories that that mind had once been thus. Then my mind could remember everything, even every word said. My mind saw everything down to the littlest detail. My young mind had early photographed what was to be learned yet that mind had been tampered with so early that behavior got in the way and created distractions along the path of learning. The feeling of not being was already strong within.

Hold still my mind. Allow expression to flow, impression to be heard. Then my mind was like a giant room, eagerly waiting to be filled, ordered, arranged, examined, and exclaimed as a wonder and a treasure. How, at this time, in this writing, I sense slightly that previous time—that time before more and more became cloud and confusion until the moment when, finally, the choice for survival came, a choice that demanded surrender of much of that mind.

It was late night on the desert as he drove me "home" or so he said.

The trembling within begins. I do not want to evoke this memory so recently freed by years of patience and gentle, steady seeking. I write in a mode that may or may not touch as deeply as the heart can bear, or be bared. Love—where was love that night? It, for sure, was not there. What thinking leads to actions of that sort?

Fear. Yes. Some. Power. Yes. Some. Desire. Yes. Some. Pain? Yes. Some. Anger? Yes. Some. Hatred? Yes. Some. Self-delusion. Yes. Some. Self-preservation? Some.

Was it a beautiful night? Yes, by some standard, yes. The stars were out bright. I, perhaps, do not want to fight. I had fought. I had struggled. I had railed at all, to all.

I was tired. It was more than that. The survival instinct continued strong. It wells up in my heart and my eyes. I cry for me. I cry for the death of me that night. Only a little longer to tell what's right, to write.

Oh, am I reticent to write? I write to free the mind, the heart, the soul. Have you ever died, yet been alive? Others have in more than just this plight. I was given no choice that night. He had played his play well. He had weakened once, not again. Even as kin of a sort, he meant it all. He would kill me if I did not heed his insistence to forget. My mind so very, very strong must will itself to forget. Confusing? But what is life? The heart soon surrendered thereafter. I keep writing. Not to write. I am not ready yet today to say what it is I am about, what I am about to say. Bear with me. The pain is so great. The road is not straight. It will come. I will be heard, I wish I could tell you of the desert that night.

I loved the desert. It was in the desert that I left myself—in the desert, there on that night. You, the reader, are, perhaps, impatient with me as you read this. Why the impatience? I do not savor the flight that I hold to so tightly. Let go; let there be light.

It was difficult to see the light that night. The night had been a very long and full night, one in which my body and mind had endured much. Closer and closer, now it comes. It is the time to tell the story, once and for all. The first time it came ever so slowly, with no sense of connection at all. There were bits and pieces, here and there, with, perhaps, months between. Often, in those months between, there seemed to be no more story to reveal. Then, later, there were months and months with no between, in which I could not bear the memories at all, yet they would not let loose of me, not in the least, not at all.

The very air I breathed was full of it all—screaming at me, screaming at me to fall. The struggle was long and triggered by events and people whose actions competed as most painful. I was a child abused by it all—by society, by family, by lies, by it all. And the repeats were strong, these triggers which added to the emotions of it all. Wounded, very wounded by it all, I sought to see it all. A feat not easily achieved with all that discontinuity and horror and mind play that told it all. Somewhere, dear God, let it be said, this is all. That's all.

Chapter 19

Ray. What about Ray? This is also a story about Ray.

It was sometime since he and Kim had moved back home to where his parents lived in northern Arizona. He waited there, not knowing what to expect. Much haunted his mind—the war, his crash, the waiting, not knowing, in and out of consciousness. The thoughts of how his father would react. What was expected of him, what the demands would be.

John, his brother, had it easier somehow. He had escaped some of his father's attention.

Well, his brother was not here now. It had all been very sudden. Suddenly, he was gone—a plane crash, a downdraft. Sudden, only enough time to turn off the engine. The plane did not ignite, but the impact was the same. The bodies did not burn, but they were all dead.

Now he faced his parents, his father alone. There was his half sister, a constant reminder of his father's transgressions.

And what of his own transgressions? Not really—he had been loyal in his marriage, no other women. Of course, there were the children, but that was not the same.

Oh, the children, what a pleasure that was. No ties really. Just pleasure. And they were so moldable, so easy to influence. He was really proud of himself how well he was able to influence them, much easier than adults, quite the opposite of his father, whom he had no influence over for good or not.

Now he had his own child. Still a baby really. And would it be the same? Probably. He was too young yet but fun to play with. Kim was recuperating from the birthing quickly. *A strong woman, I've married. She knows her place as the woman and keeps at it.*

Abstinence—hmmm, really not much opportunity lately with Kim's pregnancy and now the baby. *Ah, but that is about to change.*

Company is coming. Frances is coming. Maria is coming. Little Sonny is coming. Let's see, who will it be? All three?

Old boy, you do dream. You do flirt with yourself. It is a thought! In my own place this time. Perhaps. Perhaps.

He was looking forward to a visit from the in-laws. Amusing that it had all worked out. No messy divorce and still in the family. *And I have my own sexy woman.* Ah, yes, an interesting time.

Amazing that Chris does not suspect about his wife and the affair. That was good. *He probably doesn't want to suspect. A quick temper there—naive, gullible. I do love the jokes he tells. The best are on him.*

It was time to get ready. They would arrive soon. Would the tension be there? Would little Maria be the same as last time? She was angry.

Probably has forgotten by now the anger.

Jealousy develops early it seems.

His mind wandered back to the surprise visit to Texas, the big surprise: Guess what? I'm part of the family now.

Frances had been jealous. *I can't think of her now.* She would be around, awkward.

His mind had been wandering. Back to business. Patients were here. Back to show business, entertaining the natives, staring at big feet! *Ha. Ha. It's what they do. What I do.*

Interesting that people paid to have their feet cared for. Funny the things they told you, what a position to be in.

Ha, Ha. Behave yourself. Ray, old boy, your mind is wandering— wandering to little Maria untying her shoe.

She's the one for you and still safe too. She was quite the one last time—all over the place. But she'll soon change. She'll soon change. Why do I say that? Her resistances are funny. They charge the energies the more. No harm there.

Well, ole boy, another patient gone, and where were you? Daydreaming on the job.

He heard the baby crying next door at home. Time to help with preparations for the visit. He needed to string the lights along the front. Christmas was coming. Christmas was coming. And company was coming. And Santa better be good tonight. Ho ho and a bottle of rum. Time to prepare.

Little Maria will soon be here, and little Sonny too—a very different treat there, tender, delectable, still soft, and tiny, no knowing of what is to come. He is still an adorable little boy, a little boy to make my own. Ah, the treats of the season, ha, ha. Ole boy, you better stay away. Thinking will soon get you there, beware. Yes. Thinking will bring those pleasures near, and near they are, only a few more hours, until they are here. Pleasure, soft and dear.

There is a noise, a foot. "Kim, is that you?"

"Lunchtime, dear. Paperwork?"

"No, just wrapping up, thinking back. I miss brother John."

"It will be better. You have a son now to give to."

"There was so much I wanted to say to John. He really was upset that day, the day of the mission. Anger there, an old feud between us."

"It's over now, dear. There's nothing to be done. It's over. Come to lunch. It will be time for feeding again soon. Cheer up, we have company coming!"

Chapter 20

It was a confusing time. The trip to California seemed long. The visit to dad's brother, Dee, and his wife, Martha, was strange, tense. Many things happened, and there seemed to be much that was unclear. Aunt Martha sat in the kitchen, smoking a cigarette and talking with mother. Daddy was outside, drinking and chatting with uncle Dee, who was preparing the smoker for barbecue. He was very precise in all that he was doing. It was like the aura of the great surgeon in operation in the backyard. Barking orders to aunt Martha in the kitchen.

She touched mother's hand as she left to fetch something for uncle Dee. Mother seemed agitated, disturbed. This was strange. She seldom seemed out of control. Yesterday, there had been a big party welcoming our arrival, at least mom and dad's arrival. As kids Sonny and Maria were told that we had no business being around the adults in the evening, and were to stay put, upstairs with the nanny, and to behave. Daddy was in good form, telling jokes to everyone. Mother less so. She seemed to be suffering, somehow. Perhaps, that was what was under discussion now with aunt Martha in the kitchen.

Mother walked around the kitchen, sort of touching things as she waited for aunt Martha to return. Aunt Martha had prepared her a cup of coffee, but she didn't seem to be drinking it, more just fidgeting with the cup. She paced back and forth, waiting. Waiting for what?

The doorway from the kitchen to the living area was open. We kids had been assigned to stay in the living area so aunt Martha could keep an eye on us but still visit with mother, away from our disturbance, as she put it. Mother was sitting with her back to the door, but aunt Martha could see us directly. We could see enough to know something secretive was being discussed, something that clearly had mother agitated.

Aunt Martha returned, intent on continuing their conversation. Mother was telling aunt Martha something.

She was "so unhappy," "so confused." She was unhappy in Texas. It isn't like home to her. She confessed she had tried to leave daddy, to leave Texas while he was away but had not succeeded.

"How?" Aunt Martha asked.

"Through Ray Owen."

"I don't understand."

"Ray came to visit after his release from the VA hospital in Michigan."

"While Chris was away?"

"Yes."

"Oh."

"He was so wonderful, so attentive, so … We talked about my returning with him to Missouri."

"What about Kim?"

"Oh, he didn't even know Kim then. In fact, I introduced them, when I took him to a family party."

"When? Where?"

"Missouri."

"So, you did go back with him?"

"No, I went later, after his visit."

"When, where was Chris?"

"He was still back east, playing the invalid."

"What happened?"

"When?"

"In Missouri."

"Well, I don't know. It just didn't work out well. I didn't know what to do."

"Where was Maria?"

"Oh, she was with me. That is part of what worries me. She became strangely attached to Ray."

"How?"

"As if we were competing or something. It is really awkward, and she keeps saying inappropriate things about Ray."

"What do you mean?"

"About his, you know."

"Well, I think I understand."

Mother turned and looked to where we were playing in the living area. I quickly became very interested in what I was playing with, while playing alongside my little brother Sonny.

"Excuse me a moment, Martha."

Mother walked toward us. She picked up the toy I was playing with—a peg that was a soldier and could be put in a hole with others and pulled around. She took the toy and told me she didn't want me to play with it. "Sonny might pick it up and put it in his mouth and get hurt."

She returned to the kitchen and her visit with aunt Martha. She walked over to the kitchen door and looked out at daddy and uncle Dee.

"Perhaps, we should join the men."

It was much later that evening. Mother was sitting at aunt Martha's big piano by herself, playing at some melody. I was supposedly in bed, upstairs in the room with the window over the balcony, which looked down on the piano area below. I had never seen a window balcony inside a house before, and I loved being able to watch what was going on down below.

Suddenly, uncle Dee came into the room, went over to where mother was playing, and jerked her around at the piano. He was very angry. He yelled something about her betraying daddy. He pushed mother hard against the piano and seemed to accost mother, almost striking her. He was very, very angry. Mother tried to move away. As he swung to hit her, he hit the piano instead.

"You slut, you. Don't you ever do that to Chris again. If you do, I'll kill you with my bare hands. You little slut, life is not good enough for you with my little brother."

I was scared. I hid under the covers and put my hands up to my ears and tried really hard not to notice and fell asleep.

Chapter 21

A story told. It was a ride into darkness. The desert engulfed uncle Ray and me early. Where were we going?

Where was he taking me? I choked. I was chilled. Still shaken by the events of the evening. They seemed unending—one threat on my life after another. Broken.

It involved broken bits of my already fragile sanity.

Sanity can mean more than not madness. It can mean memory. It can mean appropriate developmental learning of the self and of society and of family and of calling and of skills and survival.

Yes, sanity can be more than "not madness." The threads of my sanity had been cut one by one in the past few hours, most rapidly. This ever so brief visit back to Arizona on our way home was to be a watershed time in my life. It was a time of the unraveling of the threads of sanity for me. And much more, it was a time of the eventual relinquishing of self—of a self strong with a destiny of its own—a self made dormant in the name of survival. A reality of a new kind was being created, not born but borne. I was in complete darkness as we drove into the desert.

The drive back to Arizona from California was again a shock to the senses. We quickly left the lush green countryside, went over mountains and into the desert on a seemingly unending drive.

It was after darkness when we arrived back in Arizona, and I was quickly put to bed. Sonny was in a portable crib bed, and I was on a narrow single bed in a tiny, narrow room. The need for sleep overcame the change of place, and morning arrived suddenly with a jolt.

I felt energized, excited again by the prospect of oranges and grapefruits on trees to be picked and enjoyed almost on the spot. This abundance brought great joy, and the warmth of the sun here seemed personal for me.

Breakfast was a feast of all my favorites, including biscuits and honey. I ate with abandon. I was beginning to really like my aunt, giving her credit for it all—the breakfast, the sunshine, the fruit bearing trees. She was joy in the morning. She would always seem so to me. That would be a memory, a feeling that held constant throughout. She was a ray of light, joy, fun, laughter, and happiness. I loved my aunt.

It was fully morning, and I as eager to get on with my day, a day eagerly anticipated and full of discovery. I was energized and looking for things to absorb, devour, and experience. It was one of those high-energy moments that adults tend to disdain and quickly grow impatient with. But as a child, I was awakening to a new world of discovery, one I was willing to meet head-on, or so it seemed.

The house was quiet. Mother, daddy, and aunt Kim were somewhere about. I could hear Ray in the bedroom with Sonny. I went in to investigate. Anger and rage and, perhaps, a tinge of jealousy built within me. Ray was playing with Sonny and, I soon sensed, in a way that I seemed to know was not right. I had seen him do it before when he visited with aunt Kim in Texas, just after Sonny's arrival from the agency at nine months and when I could not do anything to help or protect Sonny.

I was bigger now, and I sensed I could wreak havoc, if so motivated. I began to beat madly on Ray's back as he played with Sonny.

Clarity, clarity was what I needed. It was not there.

In a flash, I was being thrown to the floor. Somehow Sonny was there too, and my head was being forced down on his little body. I held my mouth closed for fear my teeth would hurt him. I gritted my teeth with all my might. I was trembling with fear, and the emotion welled up in my cheeks, neck, and throat.

I wanted to cry out, but I did not dare to cry out. The pressure from behind was so great. Now I was not only worried about hurting Sonny's little part with my teeth, but something else was happening, something to me, something I was powerless to stop.

The emotions welled up again in my neck and throat, a pain in my stomach where Sonny's foot was against me and then a shock and a horrific pain as Ray penetrated my behind again and again. The darkness of pain and horror just kept coming in waves, my heart screaming to break the cage of my body.

The pain obliterated all memories. Everything. I was gone. The shock was too much. It was too dark to know. Fleetingly, it must have been.

Then I was back and in shock. I had no idea, no memory, only Ray screaming and yelling at me. Sonny was bleeding and black and blue and crying with all his might. Ray pushed me away, causing me to fall back on the adjacent bed.

Suddenly, mother was at the door, her eyes aghast. Ray quickly explained that he had found me beating on Sonny—my own little brother.

"Perhaps, she didn't really want a baby brother after all," he said.

They took Sonny away to another room. I was left to think on what I had done. I knew only pain. I could not even cry. I couldn't tell the why of anything.

There are still questions of the mind of how this came to be, how to come back to mind, and of how this played out.

The scars are still there, at least in the mind. A visit to the doctor for colon tests sent the adult me screaming and writhing in pain. Yet there were no signs physically that anything had caused pain. I came unglued, screaming and scaring the doctor and her assistant out of their wits. They had no idea, and I did not tell them. It was too much. The tears did come and soon a glimpse of the happening. It chokes me still, leaving me again in a state of bewilderment and confusion and doubt. How could it be? How could I have done it?

Chapter 22

I am listening to poetry on the desert. Listening to strange melodic sounds on the desert. Listening to sounds of birth on the desert.

Sounds of past mourning turned to joy on the desert. The sun is rising on the desert. Maria Dee is being released from among the spirits of the long-forgotten dead. Maria Dee has at last come home. Singing and rejoicing among the spirits of long dead along the desert trail. Long they held the soul of Maria in waiting, in a death-like waiting. Now the clouds are past; the sun is rising. Singing and rejoicing among the long forgotten dead.

Maria left that night. She left and journeyed to the mountain, where the eagle spirit meets the earth spirit, to rest among the dead, long departed ancient ones. She said farewell to all that was and was to be and went to rest among the spirits of the long, departed dead to wander with them in strange symphony.

Tears for her, tears for what might have been provided dew to bless the jojoba bloom. Quiet now and still on the desert, where uncle Ray did come to kill what for him had become an ill. He came there that night to kill her.

But perhaps he could just use her will. Perhaps, it was not necessary to kill her. It was all against her will. But perhaps he could use her will to avoid the necessity to kill her.

It was clear to him now that the doctors at the hospital would not further condone the attempt to kill her, as they had seemed to do in turning a blind face to his attempt to kill Maria at the hospital. He would use his will to will her to kill her will.

Sleep now. Forget all that is past. Forget all that is past.

"Trust me. Let your mind go. Let go completely of all that is past. For I promise you that you will not see the day if you do not let the past go, if you do not will yourself to sleep."

Her soul cried out in anguish. *I want to live.*

Dear God, this choice to live was a strange choice. The choice was to live, but to live and yet not to be.

Oh, I lament and I cry. He will kill me. He will kill me. This I know. His attempts grow bolder and bolder. Dear God, I fear.

There are strange melodic sounds on the desert. Sounds of past mourning turned to awareness on the desert. Sun rising, hopes gathering, peace coming on the desert.

Maria's well is rising, rising from among the long, lonely dead. Maria's heart is freeing itself from the prisons of others' minds. Maria is coming home.

I came home to a place, new and strange, like a cleaning after the devastation of a flood, washed clear of the mementos of the past, awaiting to be cleared of the flooded debris. And so I was cleared of the flooded debris.

She awakens, as if from a dream journey both good and bad, a journey she chose originally to take in order to survive and to thrive.

Where is he? This man whose will to kill forced her will to forget, to leave her being among the long, forgotten dead, where is he?

He is gone. He can no longer cause pain, can no longer drain life from a child insisting on surviving.

Survive she did, although not ever long enough in one piece to find peace. Her mind was almost a constant split, knowing it was too dangerous to remain, to retain even a glimpse of memory of all this in order to survive.

The sun is rising on the desert. Maria is being brought back from among the spirits of the long-forgotten dead. Maria is, at last, coming home. Singing and rejoicing among the spirits of the long dead, along the desert trail.

A few years ago at Christmastime, going to Arizona for the holidays, my husband and I planned an overnight. We would stay in northern Arizona, allowing us to have a rental car for the drive south and some independence within a family visit. As the plane neared Phoenix, I looked forward toward the Superstitions Mountains. We had to go there early tomorrow, but I didn't know why. For sometime, I'd had a fear. I was soon to die—it was just a fear—and I did not want to die.

We dove there before the sun shone above the mountains and walked among the jojoba on the hills. It was there the memory again came—the memory of that night when Ray drove out into the desert with his intent that I die. It was there that I faced the fear that I might die and that I must not remember. And it was there that I'd had to direct my will to survive, by not remembering.

There had been a fire on the desert the winter before, and only charred remains remained—skeletons of the past. Signs of new growth were few. Now that four more years had passed, the desert was beginning to bloom—newly so. It wasn't the same as before, for what had been before was gone, only a charred skeleton of the past. But new growth was beginning to bloom, yet ever so mindful of the past.

Oh, hush, hush, my child. Do not sleep, the sleep of the past. Stay awake, stay awake, my child. You must keep constant vigil, if you are to allay the past. Awake, my child. Sing, sing a song of the heart, that you be not forgetful of the past, that you may at last pass through what is past.

Chapter 23

What is past is past, but the story has still more to be told. It is not over yet, this saga of terror and horror. It begs for the entire story to be told. I would skip a day, perhaps a year, perhaps a lifetime rather than tell the story to be told. But I must not. It is my freeing to tell the story that is to be told.

There is much that is not remembered. The occurrences come each on their own, triggered by some present event or punctuated by some physical ailment, strangely not treatable. Yet, once remembered and revisited and, at many levels, released, the mystery ailment would slip away, no longer noted unless some symbolic occurrence occurred.

As I was being sodomized by my uncle that special, sunny morning, my left foot was pinned down by the thrust and power of my uncle's body.

For almost ten years before the memory was released, I had difficulty with shooting pains in my left foot. The pain would engage more and more of my leg, so that, at last, I had to sit down, keeping my leg up, until the muscle relaxed. Podiatrist visits and chiropractic adjustments brought but temporary relief. It was suggested the nerve ending be clipped somehow, so that I would not feel it when the trigger point was engaged. I noticed that going without shoes could trigger it in a walk from the bathroom to the bedroom, so I soon quit going without shoes for even a few steps. Nothing seemed to stop it, and it did not seem to have any rhyme or rhythm to it, other than I felt susceptible when without shoes.

After the memory of the sodomy was experienced, I began to be aware that the foot pain was seldom triggered and, when it was, was much less severe. It was noted, by someone unaware of my story, that the pain seemed to come on when I was feeling "pinned down" or felt I was being forced to do something I did not want to do.

I go without shoes around the house and up and down stairs, always marveling that such a simple pleasure has returned.

Chapter 24

My story, this story is very difficult to tell. It means walking back into that dark room of the past.

A voice somewhere inside says, "Yes, it lets in the light. And in the light, the evil of the past cannot survive; cannot grow; cannot fester away at your heart, your soul, your very being."

So, I write, even though, on some levels, I do not want to write. It is not the writing, per se. It is what comes forth and what it stirs and the aftermath of the writing, when I grasp to stay somehow centered.

The message still comes through—that I must write in spite of the pain and angst. I must write because of the pain and angst.

There is still confusion within my logical mind as to time. Was it later that day? Was it the next day? Was there the break of the visit to California between incidents?

Sequential memory was so very grossly abused because of the various events. Departures and gaps in memory about because of the inability to stay in the mind while things beyond the imagination of a child were, in reality, happening to a child.

Sometime after the incident with Sonny, when the shock of the event seemed to blur—even memory of previous encounters with Ray, in fact, any memory of the previous history of molestation and seduction, and even the awareness of mother's culpability had blurred—Maria naively walked into the bedroom where Ray's baby boy had been moved during the visit. It was a room with a double bed in it as well. Maria was looking with curiosity at the sleeping baby boy so tiny and cute.

Uncle Ray entered the room.

"Well, what have we here? Uncle Ray's sweet little Maria Dee and his very own baby boy."

Ray closed the door, saying, he didn't want the baby to be disturbed and moved toward Maria and the baby bed, thus trapping Maria between the baby bed and the double bed. Maria moved away from the baby bed so that Ray could see the baby and sat on the edge of the bed. Ray did not seem too interested in his baby son at the moment.

"Now, how is my pretty little niece this morning? You are all recuperated and feeling okay? You know your uncle Ray was not trying to hurt you yesterday?"

Maria Dee did not understand and looked down at her lap in embarrassment. She was unaccustomed to not comprehending what was being said. She started to look elsewhere, feeling queasy and uneasy but not sure why.

"Come here, my sweet child. Come to your uncle Ray. Show me all is forgiven, that you are my sweet, dear Maria Dee."

Maria sat, puzzled further. She did not know what to do. Uncle Ray seemed to be getting agitated.

He suddenly unbuckled his belt and lowered his pants. Something was sticking out. Maria was panicked. She did not know what was happening. She did not know what to do. She inched up on the bed, hoping to get around uncle Ray and scramble off the bed and out of the room.

Her dress was askew as she tried to move on the cotton ribbing of the cover on the bed. Ray did not wait. He grabbed her, forcing her back upon the top of the bed, hitting her head against the wall. She was frightened. She didn't know what was happening. Ray was pinning her down, holding her arms down with an elbow on one arm and his hand on the other arm, while he fumbled with her underpants. She struggled, trying to kick him and break loose, but she could not move.

"Why, you little bitch, you know you want this."

He pressed down on her, biting her lip, and pushing himself against her, until she could feel something terrible inside her, tearing at her skin. She cried and struggled, trying to move, but his body was too big, too heavy. She could not fight him. She began to cry. She felt like she was being punished for something somehow, and she did not understand what or why.

Ray was clearly angry with her, but she did not know why. And why would he do what he had just done? Why would he punish her? The pain inside continued. Why was he hurting her so? He finally stopped. She still did not know what to do or why he had done what he had done.

He moved off her, cautiously, aware she had stopped her struggle. She was holding very, very still, paralyzed with fear, not knowing what to expect, what he might do.

He held her down with his arm still, while he reached for his pants with his other arm, awkwardly slipping back into them. After yesterday, he did not trust her not to strike at him. He was aware something was going to have to be done. She seemed really almost unaware of what was going to happen today and continued resisting throughout. He had better think quickly about this, or there was bound to be trouble. As his mind wandered, his grip on Maria loosened.

She sprung immediately from the bed; ran out of the room and out the front door, tripping over the hose as she rounded the side of the house; and fell into the wet and the mud.

She was crying and frightened when her mother found her. Taking her cautiously by the arm to avoid getting herself wet and muddy, she let Maria into the house and down the hall to the bathroom.

"Here, sit on the toilet while I run you a bath and get you some clean clothes." She could not imagine what had gotten into Maria Dee. Why was she behaving this way? Why was she so upset?

Chapter 25

She was bathing Maria Dee, her mind wandering all the while. She was glad she had spoken with her sister-in-law, Martha. Doing so had seemed to release a cloud that had hung about her. Although she had not expected that Martha would tell her husband. *I must watch that. Perhaps it would be safer to keep all this to myself.* At that moment, the telling had released something.

Maria Dee needs to talk it seems. I don't like what she is saying. She is always fantasizing and saying bad things about good people. She needs to learn not to do that.

Now she was saying something about Ray. Why would Ray do what she was suggesting? What would Ray want with kids? He had Kim.

And he could have had me. He is such a dear, wonderful man. She really mustn't say these things.

"Now, what were you saying?"

"Daddy. He did to me what daddy, what daddy does to you."

Rage welled up in Frances. What could she be saying? When had her daughter been aware of Chris and her?

"See. He hurt me, here." Maria Dee was pointing to between her legs as she sat in the tub, in the water.

Frances paused. She slowly dropped the sponge. She could not believe what she was seeing. The area Maria was pointing to was all red. But it couldn't be what she had said. *She is lying. She hurt herself playing with herself. She must stop this destructive lying. She could hurt us all, even talking about Chris's and my togetherness. I must put a stop to this. I must.*

"Maria Dee, you are lying. Ray did not do this. You did this to yourself. Here, I'll show you what it feels like. You won't say lies again. You hear me. I'll show you."

And with that, Frances began pushing two of her fingers up Maria's vagina again and again and again.

Was it anger? Was it recognition? Was it jealousy? Was it disbelief? Was it a feeling of lack of control?

It didn't matter. With that outburst and infliction upon Maria by her mother, Maria had gone far, far away in time and space. The shock of the invasion, the pain, and the horror were just too much. The need to escape was far beyond anything else that had happened.

Maria Dee split from the body. She was standing there in the room, looking at Frances and at what Frances was doing to her body. She would stay out of that body. She would stand on her own. She would not be hurt this way again. She would protect herself. She would stay away from her mother. She would distance herself. She would stand on her own. She would be free from this body and these attachments.

When she came to, she was in her bed in her nightgown. It was afternoon. She did not know how long she had been there or why she was in bed in her nightclothes in the afternoon. She decided to stay there to gather herself together.

Usually she was sent to bed early when she had, in some way, annoyed mother or daddy. But this was late afternoon. Why was she there?

Then she remembered what Ray had done to her and what her mother had said and done. She was very sore. She put her hand between her thighs and fell back to sleep.

She awakened to find daddy and aunt Kim by the bed—aunt Kim with food, daddy standing nearby. They were very quiet. All was very quiet, as aunt Kim encouraged Maria to eat.

"You had a nasty fall today. Here, this soup will give you strength. You just stay here and rest. Your mom and dad and I are going out to a party, but your uncle will check in on you from time to time."

"We're going home in the morning," daddy said.

Home? Home? Why was the pain so strong in my heart? Home? I did not feel that anywhere was home. A tear hit the pillow as I once again fell asleep.

I feel devastated, as if I was down in a well and enchained with no escape.

It is overwhelming sometimes, this feeling of being in an abyss. How, how am I to go back and forth, between today and then? I feel trapped in between nowhere in the well.

That feeling of being in the well and the feeling before any memories were attached was one of the first things my therapist and I worked on in therapy—trying to experience a way out of the well. At last, I sensed escape from the well by dropping into the water and floating away. I was washed away out of the well in a sea of my tears that, held inside, had kept me in the well.

Once, there was a huge body of salty water, giving me buoyancy to be washed over, to float away, and to land out of the well.

As I write this, I am once again able to leave the feeling of being in the well.

Chapter 26

It was sometime after dark. I had been sleeping a deep, tired sleep. I did not hear him enter the room. I did not sense his removing the covers on the bed. I was suddenly shocked into awakening as he lay on top of my legs and buttocks. His private part pressed against me. His hands were gripping my bottom. In an instant, I knew this time to struggle and to fight.

My awakening caught him off guard. I started struggling to break free and to turn over so as to face him, where I might have some defense against his actions and to keep him from penetrating my rear end.

I turned over and came around with fists clinched and pounded on his chest as best I could. I broke free but to no avail. I was in the dark, and he was standing in front of the door. To my surprise, my hitting him evoked something in him, and he began hitting and punching me in the stomach and chest.

I started screaming, "I'll tell aunt Kim. I'll tell aunt Kim."

"Oh, no you don't," he said as he put his hand over my mouth. I bit him.

This angered him more. He grabbed my arm, jerking me out of bed.

"I've had enough of this. You're coming with me," he said.

He pulled me by the arm and knocked things out of the way as he dragged me in my nightgown and bare feet through the living room and kitchen and out into the garage.

I kept trying to grab onto anything I could to stop his progress. He stopped and shook me by the shoulders, saying he would take care of me now.

He continued pulling me into the garage and holding me by the arm all the while. The garage was filled with boxes, garden equipment, and stuff. The light was dim and only lit faintly. He seemed to be searching for something. He grabbed boxes and dumped out contents, saying bad words all the while.

Finally, he dumped one box that had a pack of some sort like daddy had from the military. He began fishing through it. He dumped stuff out on the floor and pushed it all around to look through it. It was a cold and damp feeling on the floor, and my feet were cold.

"I'm cold. My feet are cold," I cried.

He ignored me, still intent upon his search. Suddenly he reached back into the now empty pack and said he had found it. He pulled something very small out of the bottom of the pack. He then tried to adjust his grip on me. I broke loose, and started to run back to the house, where I hoped to get in a room and lock the door until mother, daddy, and aunt Kim came home.

But as I moved barefoot through the stuff on the floor, I tripped over the hose, which was lying across the floor.

It scared me. I thought it was a snake. It was just enough for him to grab me again. By now, my heart was pounding with fear. I did not know what to do. He pinned me down on the cold floor and forced the pill that he was holding into my mouth, forcing me to swallow it.

"This will take care of you," I remember hearing him say as I began to drift away.

Then the nightmares began, and my body was a mass of sweat. I was shaking from head to toe uncontrollably. I was jerking around and around, screaming all the while. I was out of control. My head felt as if it would burst. I was hysterical. This seemed to have a strange effect on uncle Ray. My entire body was in convulsions.

Next thing I knew I was in a hospital room, and there were doctors. They were putting a tube in me, and I was convulsing. I have no words to express what was happening to me. I was making strange sounds and rocking back and forth, convulsing. My head felt crazy and then gone, and then it would happen again. I felt like my lungs would burst. They were giving me a shot of something.

Uncle Ray was telling the doctors that I had gotten into his old army survival kit and swallowed his emergency pill. He was telling them that I was a very precocious child, tending toward mischief.

"No," I tried to cry out, barely able to communicate. "No." I was becoming very groggy.

"No. He did it."

But they did not seem to hear me. He heard me and quickly distracted them and held me down saying, "She seems to be falling asleep."

One of the doctors said, "She's had a rough time, but the worst seems past. You got her here in the nick of time. A few more minutes, and she would have been a goner. You better check that garage for hazards, now that you have a kid of your own."

The doctors seemed to know uncle Ray. They seemed to be leaving the room. While they were there, I felt safe from uncle Ray, even though he'd lied to them and distracted them from hearing me.

I tried to reach out and to cry out, "Please don't leave me alone."

They seemed to think I was being delusionary, as they called it, and decided I best be tied down so that I would do myself no harm until all the effects of the pill had worn off and the drugs took effect.

I struggled, trying to tell them. But they only tried to calm me down. I was petrified at being left alone and defenseless with uncle Ray.

"We'll check in on her in a little while, to see if her heart rate has settled down. When she's stable, you can take her home."

They left the room, leaving me alone with uncle Ray. Groggy from what they had given me, I fought to stay awake, fearful and known that I must stay awake, lest uncle Ray try something else. And try he did.

Almost as soon as they had left the room, he started fussing with the bed linens and the pillows. I rocked back and forth, trying to keep awake. But they had strapped my arms down so I could not move well, and my lower body felt especially weak from the pill, the convulsions, and the "purge" as they called it. I wanted to fall asleep and to let go. The pull was very strong. I fought it, but the pull to sleep kept getting stronger.

Then he made his move. He slowly lifted a pillow over my face. I struggled but could not resist. I tried to cry out.

"Shush, shush," he kept saying. "Don't fight it, just go to sleep."

I tried to hold my breath, as if he could not take it away that way. I tried to lie very still in hopes he would quit pressing down. It was like being in a nightmare. I wanted to cry out but couldn't. I couldn't be heard, and at the same time, I was holding my breath and holding my body still so that he might let loose. At the same time, I was fighting the medication. Deep within me, the horrors kept striking at me, tearing me apart. The cries not screamed and screamed deep within me are there still today.

Those screams—the feeling of being suffocated, the feeling of holding on, the feeling of horror, and more feelings than words can express—have demanded attention again and again with great strength as life incidents have triggered a sense of déjà vu.

The helplessness was miraculously given light. At least for the moment, there was hope. Footsteps could be heard down the hall, and uncle Ray suddenly flung the pillow across the room in an attempt to distance himself from the offense.

I was without voice and without strength to cry out. Tears ran down my cheeks. Uncle Ray was seen wiping them off as the nurse and a doctor entered the room. There was a moment when the nurse picked up the pillow and looked at the doctors, who seemed puzzled and then shook their heads, as if to say, "No. It couldn't be. He's one of us."

"Let's get this child out of here and on her way home" the nurse said gently, soothingly, as if attempting to comfort me with her words.

"'That will be the best thing for her. She is going back to Texas tomorrow, one of the doctors asked?"

"Yes."

"Well, if she takes it easy, she should be okay by the time she gets home. There's really nothing more that we can do for her here. Do you want us to call the house, to let them know that you two are on your way home?"

"No, that won't be necessary. I'll make the call on our way out. Thank you, doctors and Sally, very much. Sorry to have caused any inconvenience. Sure serves as a warning to get that garage cleaned out before little Bobby starts crawling. Thanks again. Your support has been tremendous. I'm sure Maria Dee won't forget this night for a long time to come."

"Ray, good to see you. We'll have a chair round for you in just a few minutes. That will give the young lady a few more minutes to rest before you take her home. She has more color in her face already. Good. Take care of yourself, young lady. You're mighty lucky to have such a smart uncle nearby to come to your rescue!" the doctor smiled at Maria.

I rested back, feeling safe for the moment. They had removed the restraints. I dozed off. Then I was awakened, aware they were trying to move me onto the wheelchair. I struggled and fought to stay on the bed.

"Time to go home, young lady."

I did not want to go home. I fought to resist being moved to the chair.

"She's had a rough night of it" said Ray. No wonder she doesn't want to go home! She'll be okay, once she gets home to her own bed. One more trip, dear. Then you can rest all you want."

I kept looking back as I was shuttled to the front door of the hospital. Uncle Ray passed the telephones without stopping. When we got to the car, I resisted being removed from the wheelchair. I did not want to be alone with uncle Ray. Not on your life. The nurses laid me across the backseat of the small car.

Uncle Ray got in the front, and we drove away into the night and into the desert. I dozed off.

The next thing I remember, uncle Ray had reached over the backseat. He had his hand between my legs. He was very gently massaging my private parts. He started saying sweet things to me, how I was his dear, precious child; that he would never hurt me; and that he loved me. It was like it was before when he had given me attention. I slowly was filled with desire for him, wanting his affection and his touch.

Why was he doing all this to me? Why? I was very weak, just lying there in the backseat, yet somehow aroused by his touch. He moved to the backseat, where he continued caressing and saying gentle things to me. This was a Ray I remembered, loved. He made love to me tenderly, and I was his.

"Don't make me go home. Please."

He became alert, suddenly responding, "Maria Dee, you must go home. You must forget all about this."

"No, no. I don't want to."

"Maria Dee, you must go home. You must forget all about this."

My heart was torn and too weary to resist. I had been worn down at last by his touch, his attention, and his gentleness. He was saying that I must go home and that I must forget all this. My heart was torn. He kissed my eyes and caressed my hair as tears ran down my face.

"Maria Dee, you must go home. You must forget all about this. Otherwise, you know that I must kill you. You have no more protection. You are alone, and you will die.

"I must kill you. You know this, don't you? Look at me. You know this. You know that I must kill you. You know this, don't you?"

He forced my face to look into his. His face was quiet and calm. There was no wavering.

I knew what he said to be true. I felt sure he would kill me as we drove into the desert. I knew that I had no defense but to surrender, and surrender I had. It was a bittersweet surrender, accepting what was his to give and in the end feeling my heart break from within.

I surrendered, understanding that I must forget and that only in forgetting for real would I have a chance to survive.

Only if he truly believed that I had forgotten would I survive, and so even as my mind fought doing so, I forgot. I forgot all about the past. I forgot all about uncle Ray playing with me, playing with mother, and playing with Sonny. I forgot all about being in the hospital. I forgot all about what had been done to me. I was only to remember that my wonderful uncle Ray loved me, that he was my special uncle, and that he was very fond of me.

My mind and I made a pact for me to forget and to never stay long enough together to get caught, even as my mind and I fought. I knew it was for naught, that indeed we must never get caught remembering. And so a massive net fell over me, weighing me down and keeping the sun from shining in on my mind. I was ever careful not to be caught remembering.

My head hurts from the writing of this. My heart cries from the remembering of this—more in the heart still than in the mind. The mind had wound tight for so very, very long with the forgetting in order to survive. Such fear it takes to keep from remembering, such danger in remembering.

My mind is still not the same, even in remembering. It's like a prisoner of war, returning after so very many years in isolation. Those years are gone, those memories do not exist, and a whole child was not there—to grow up a whole adult. The adult now works with what remains, hoping to build strength and courage in that eight-year-old child who has come out at last. She's hopeful of finding joy

in what is left and not being bitter or too damaged to grow some
before it is too late.

Three months later, uncle Ray sent an Easter bunny almost as
tall as Maria Dee, with a note reminding her that her wonderful
uncle Ray loved her, that he was her special uncle, reminding her
to forget.

Ray did not leave it all to Maria Dee to forget. He somehow
convinced Maria's mother that it was best for Maria to forget as
much as possible. For the safety of both their marriages and without
explaining how or why, Ray taught Maria's mother a saying and a
rubbing of the temples that would calm Maria and help her to forget.
And so Maria's mother helped Maria to forget.

My last memory of the entire trip was on the drive home. I
sensed I had surrendered all. I placed my hand and my life in my
mother's with all my own hopes, desires, and dreams. My heart and
my memories were left at rest in the desert. I surrendered my all to
her. No more was my own being seldom seen at all except when a
rebel personality was somehow in charge.

When many, many years later thoughts of suicide erupted upon
my own initiative to live far away from mother, my being began
to reemerge. The strength of the ties began to unravel and left me
feeling I had no life of my own.

Postscript

And now, after many, many, many years of bits and pieces and being away, I've come to gather the pieces and retrace the steps of the journeys I was sent upon by the visitor's visits to my inner world.

I gather these pieces up in my hands and look at them as a stranger would look upon a shell found on a beach; it's difficult to recognize the once gloriously alive and radiant creature I once was.

I've never been here before—as I pick up the pieces, the vision worlds I missed, and the castles in the sky I might have known had not a visitor visited.

I've never been here before to smell the roses. I am being born as Christ with Mary, I to a new mother. And pure, I am born.

Footnotes

Maria's mother is now suffering her own memory loss and journeys away. Maria has journeyed away across the country with her own guardian angel-spouse in search of her house, her home at home, her life, and their life. And so, in a real sense, she has never been here before. Her uncle has passed away.

An adult intelligence test revealed a much lower reading for the categories of "short-term memory" and "picture completion" than the rest of her very high IQ.

She also has an eye floater and lung issues as a result of the attempt on her life at the hospital, and it took years for her to learn how to breathe properly.

Notes from Maria

Roses are the symbol of the heart and of having a heart. I had no sense of heart. I had no sense of heart all those years. For years, I saw my heart as locked in my mother's imperfect heart. There were years of no heart.

Roses are the symbol of the heart. And so this year, I seek *roses* of the heart, a new heart, my heart—soft, beautiful, gently fragrant pink roses of the heart.

I bought myself three exquisitely beautiful, soft pink roses—expensive roses at five dollars a stem. The cost of these roses is nothing for a heart to pay in order to play.

Twice, my husband has brought me pink roses, each a little richer in color than the last.

Now I paint roses, beautiful roses, red and golden roses too, symbols of a spiritual path.

Printed in the United States
By Bookmasters